Functional Assessment of Academic Behavior

JAMES
YSSELDYKE,
PH.D.

SANDRA
CHRISTENSON,
PH.D.

*Creating
Successful Learning
Environments*

ISBN 1-57035-512-6

10 11 12 13 14 FRD 19 18 17 16 15

Printed in the United States of America
Published and Distributed by

Sopris West™
EDUCATIONAL SERVICES

A Cambium Learning Company

4093 Specialty Place • Longmont, Colorado 80504
303.651.2829 • www.sopriswest.com

25697/168FAAB/2-15

Jim Ysseldyke, Ph.D., is Professor of Educational Psychology and Associate Dean for Research in the College of Education and Human Development at the University of Minnesota. From 1983-1989 Ysseldyke was Director of the Minnesota Institute for Research on Learning Disabilities, and from 1990-1999 he was Director of the National Center on Educational Outcomes.

Ysseldyke completed his undergraduate work at Calvin College and Western Michigan University and taught disturbed and delinquent youth for two years in Grand Rapids, Michigan. He completed masters and doctoral degrees in school psychology at the University of Illinois and worked as a school psychologist in Michigan.

Ysseldyke's research and writing have focused on issues in assessing and making instructional decisions about students with disabilities. He is an author of four major textbooks: *Introduction to Special Education*; *Assessment*; *Critical Issues in Special Education*; and *The Challenge of Complex School Problems*. He has published book chapters, journal articles, an instructional environment scale (*TIES-II*), and a teacher evaluation scale. He is conducting a set of investigations on the use of accelerated math to enhance instructional outcomes for students in urban environments. Ysseldyke has received awards for his research from the School Psychology Division of the American Psychological Association, the American Educational Research Association, and the Council for Exceptional Children. The University of Minnesota presented him a Distinguished Teaching Award, and he received a Distinguished Alumni Award from the University of Illinois. From 1986-1992 Ysseldyke served as Editor of *Exceptional Children*, the journal of the Council for Exceptional Children.

Sandra L. Christenson received her Ph.D. from the University of Minnesota and is currently Professor of Educational and Child Psychology there. Her research is focused on (1) interventions that enhance student engagement with school and learning, and (2) identification of contextual factors that facilitate student engagement and increase the probability for student success in school. She is particularly interested in populations that are most alienated from traditional schooling practices and/or at highest risk for nonschool completion. Her recent investigations are aimed at understanding how students make a personal investment in learning and ways to promote the role of families in educating students. Christenson has published extensively about theory, research, and strategies for engaging parents in school and learning. She has served on several editorial boards and is section editor for *School Psychology Quarterly* and coeditor for the book series, *Applying Psychology to the Schools*. Christenson was the 1992 recipient of the Lightner Witmer Award from APA for scholarship and early career contributions to the field of school psychology.

CONTENTS

Identifying a Student's Instructional Needs, Our History

In 1988, we published *TIES: The Instructional Environment Scale* because we believed no assessment is complete without an assessment of instruction and development of an intervention plan. We were concerned that assessment practices focused too much on placement—**where** the student would receive instruction as opposed to focusing on the critical concept of an appropriate assessment-to-intervention link—or **what would occur** during instruction regardless of the specific placement. We were concerned about the quantity and quality of instruction across the school day for referred students. We knew that placement in a particular program, classroom, or service delivery system was not necessarily an intervention. And, we believed an effective intervention must create a person-environment fit that affords the referred student opportunities to be engaged in academically relevant tasks with a high degree of success. The instructional environment in *TIES* was the classroom context, whether in general or special education or a Title I classroom or small group supplemental tutoring format.

In 1993, we extended the concept of instructional environment to include both classroom and home contexts. We also changed the name of the tool from a "scale" to a "system" for gathering data on both the instructional and home environments. *The Instructional Environment System-II (TIES-II)* emphasized evidence-based instructional and home factors that assist student learning. The focus was largely on understanding the instructional needs for a student about whom educators and parents were concerned.

Thirteen years since the original publication and our call for examining a student's instructional environment and addressing a student's specific instructional needs, *Functional Assessment of Academic Behavior (FAAB)* is developed. Clearly, the interest in achieving a good match between the learner and the environment has grown. In fact, interventionists are now particularly interested in alterable factors that make a difference in student progress and learning. *FAAB* maintains a focus on identifying and coordinating instructional, home, and home-school supports for the referred student with the express purpose of designing feasible interventions to enhance the student's academic success. We define success in terms of student progress and engagement; therefore, a student is successful if he/she learns more today than he/she did yesterday.

In *FAAB* we draw on the concept of functional assessment because we are interested in identifying antecedents in the student's total learning environment that lead to positive consequences for student learning, namely student engagement and progress in school. It is a system that is focused on clarifying the presence or absence of **environmental** conditions that enhance a student's academic success and progress in school. *FAAB* adds an essential piece to conducting functional assessment of student academic behavior. Some functional assessments focus exclusively on describing student characteristics in the classroom and the factors that maintain student behavior, particularly problematic behavior. *FAAB* adds a structure for examining evidence-based factors that predict greater academic success. No functional assessment is complete without a focus on the supports to maintain the positive performance of students. Others have agreed with us regarding this point. For example, Freeman and Smith (2001) stated, "It is critical to attend to variables that will increase the 'contextual fit' between an individual's behavior support plan and those who implement the plan" (p. 6). With the use of *FAAB*, educators and parents can begin to answer: Under what type of conditions does the student perform most optimally? We developed a system that considers the person-environment fit for learning over time.

We are absolutely committed to the belief that the bottom line in assessment is improvement of outcomes for individual students. Also, we believe students need supportive learning environments to demonstrate optimal personal success. Thus, assessment is not mutually exclusive of intervention. Rather, assessment is a continuous process in which implementing an intervention generates more information as to the conditions under which the student's response is optimal. It is our hope that users of *FAAB* find it of considerable assistance in organizing the vast array of contextual influences as they design interventions aimed at improving the progress and performance of individual students.

OVERVIEW OF THE MANUAL

The *FAAB* manual is organized into four sections: (Chapter 1) The What, Why, When, and Where of *FAAB*; (Chapter 2) How to Use *FAAB*; (Chapter 3) Using *FAAB* Results to Plan Interventions; and the Appendix.

In Chapter 1, users are introduced to 23 alterable variables associated with positive academic performance and categorized as instructional support for learning, home support for learning, and home-school support for learning. These variables are used to change learning environments so that the student is responding to instruction more positively. It is essential to assess a student's instructional needs in context to enhance the student's opportunity to learn, to identify the many factors that influence school success, and to provide instructionally relevant information to teachers and parents. *FAAB* is particularly helpful to prereferral or intervention assistance teams and in individual parent-teacher consultations about a student's academic performance. It is used when questions asked about the referred student are: "How can educators and parents create the most optimal conditions for this student's learning?" or

"Under what conditions or with what kinds of instructional supports for learning does the student perform most optimally?"

In Chapter 2, nine steps important in the assessment and intervention planning process are described. These steps provide a structure for intervention planning for the referred student to make a more successful adaptation to classroom instruction. They help parents and teachers determine what contextual changes can be made to improve the student's performance. The steps, which are consistent with problem solving assessment and consultation models, are:

► Identify and Clarify the Referral Concern

► Understand the Student's Instructional Needs From the Perspective of the Teacher and the Parents

► Collect Data on the Student's Instructional Environment

► Prioritize and Plan Interventions to Meet the Student's Instructional Needs

► Identify Ways for Home Support for Learning

► Implement the Intervention

► Evaluate the Effectiveness of the Instructional Intervention

► Revise the Intervention Plan

► Document the Intervention and Report Results

Different ecological assessment methods are described in this section as well.

In Chapter 3, examples of interventions designed to enhance instructional supports for learning, home supports for learning, and home-school supports for learning are provided. In keeping with the notion of individualized and contextualized assessment and intervention planning, users are encouraged to trust their knowledge of student behavior and performance and to create other interventions. In particular, the educational professionals and parents who know the student in this context best, should make judgments about the quality, intensity, and frequency of interventions to achieve greater academic success for the student. And, the critical step of evaluating and documenting the effectiveness of interventions is underscored, because we know that empirically supported interventions do not always work for all students.

The Appendix consists of five required *FAAB* forms and six supplemental forms. Users of *FAAB* have permission to reproduce the forms. Users should select the forms that are relevant for addressing the needs of the student about whom they are concerned. The reproducible forms are:

FUNCTIONAL
ASSESSMENT OF
ACADEMIC
BEHAVIOR

► The *Instructional Environment Checklist*-This form consists of 23 support for learning components that are associated with academic success for students. It is used to select priority areas for intervention planning by school personnel familiar with ecological influences on student learning.

▶ The *Instructional Environment Checklist: Annotated Version*-This form delineates the indicators for each of the 23 support for learning components that are associated with academic success for students. This version is used to select priority areas for intervention planning by school personnel who require greater detail about the ecological influences on student learning.

▶ The *Instructional Needs Checklist*-This form provides information on the teacher's observations of the student under different instructional conditions. Systematic gathering of data related to the teacher's experiences with the student helps to clarify the referral concern.

▶ *Parental Experience With Their Child's Learning and Schoolwork*-This form provides information on the parents' (or caregivers') perspective on the student's responses to instruction and learning. It provides an efficient way to gather information about the student's instructional history across school years and to actively involve the parent(s) in the assessment and intervention planning process.

▶ The *Intervention Documentation Record*-This form provides an efficient way for educators to keep track across school years of the interventions that have been implemented and their effectiveness.

Six additional forms are provided to assist educators about the method for collecting data and the kinds of data to be collected. These forms were used in *TIES-II* and are included here because they may be instructive for individuals becoming familiar with doing an ecological assessment of student's instructional needs. We recognize that many users of *FAAB* will not need to refer to these data gathering forms.

▶ The *Observation Record* is used to collect data on the student's performance and behavior relevant to instructional support for learning. It maintains the focus of the observation on the student in relation to the task characteristics and instruction and management strategies used in the classroom.

▶ The *Student Interview Record* provides a semi-structured interview format that allows the examiner to gather information on the student's perspective of his/her learning experience, specifically the assigned task during the classroom observation and assignments during the last month.

▶ The *Teacher Interview Record* provides a semi-structured interview format that allows the examiner to gather information about the student's instruction that may not be readily observable. The focus is on understanding the teacher's experience instructing the student.

▶ The *Parent Interview Record* provides a structure for gathering information about parent expectations and attributions, discipline strategies, parent-child interactions in general and around schoolwork, parent participation in schooling, and the structure provided for learning in the home. The tone of the interview is very conversational and allows parents to select the best way for them to support their child's learning.

▶ *Supplemental Teacher Interview Questions* for each of the 12 instructional support for learning components are provided to illustrate the different ways to gather information about instructional conditions that affect student performance. Examiners are encouraged to reword and create other questions.

▶ *Supplemental Student Interview Questions* for each of the 12 instructional support for learning components are provided to illustrate the different ways to gather information about the student's experience with learning. Examiners are encouraged to reword and create other questions.

Users who are less familiar with ecological assessment and intervention planning, specifically literatures on effective instruction, home influences on students' learning and development, and the importance of the congruence and continuity across home and school contexts, will find the references at the end of the manual to be very informative.

CHAPTER 1

The What, Why, When, and Where of FAAB

THE "WHAT" OF FAAB

No student assessment can be considered complete without an assessment of the student's instructional needs in context. This contention appears so obvious that few would disagree with it. Yet, in practice, most psychoeducational decisions for a student are made without careful, systematic analysis of the instructional environment. It is essential to identify school and home influences that predict and maintain the student's level of academic performance *(Ysseldyke & Christenson, 1993, p.1 of preface).*

When students are not making sufficient academic progress, many times discussions center on the structural aspects of instruction such as lengthening the school day or year, offering all day kindergarten, or retention (Slavin, Karweit, & Wasik, 1994). The quality of the instructional program and the educational resources (what we think of as supports for learning) during these structural changes for students are far too often missing from the discussion. According to Slavin and his colleagues, it is not the structure per se that is most important for student learning but rather what goes on during the structure provided. Thus, the student's opportunity to learn does not depend solely on availability of time. It also depends on the quality of the instructional program and educational resources available. Similarly, a student's competency in one learning environment does not mean competency in another learning environment. While the list of instructional interventions has expanded considerably in the past two decades, an intervention is only as good as how it is implemented. Interventionists must pay attention to context, because the power of an intervention is reduced substantially if the contextual supports are not in place. *FAAB* assists professionals in organizing the contextual influences for individual students, mobilizing resources to enhance appropriate student responding, and focusing on quality of the instructional opportunity for the student.

Conceptual Framework

Based on the systems-ecological framework for children's development proposed by Bronfenbrenner (1979), the **instructional environment** is defined broadly to include those contexts in which learning takes place (school, classrooms, homes) as well as the interface of essential contexts for children's learning (home-school relationship). Drawing from the seminal work of Bronfenbrenner, we conceptualize the instructional environment in *FAAB* as including school, home, and home-school contexts (see *Figure 1*).

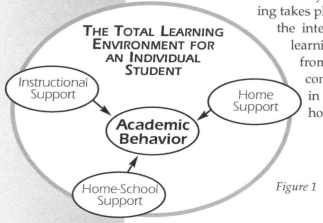

THE TOTAL LEARNING ENVIRONMENT FOR AN INDIVIDUAL STUDENT

Instructional Support

Home Support

Academic Behavior

Home-School Support

Figure 1

It is important for educators and parents to understand the concept of the **total learning environment** (see *Figure 2*), the powerful effect of both home and school on the student's learning.

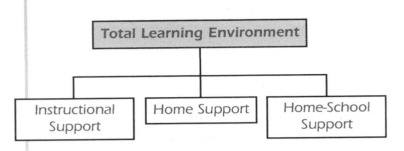

Figure 2

Much is known about the kinds of factors that promote positive learning outcomes. How the student spends his/her time in-school and out-of-school in relation to school tasks must be in accord with these support-for-learning factors if we are to achieve optimal learning outcomes. Students who extend their learning on school-relevant tasks to out-of-school hours without a doubt perform better than those who do not choose to or have few opportunities to do so (Clark, 1990). Furthermore, the degree of continuity in messages between home and school to the student about such things as the value of school and learning, use of time, and persistence in the face of challenging tasks must be considered. The home-school relationship is a variable that enhances or inhibits students' performance and progress within and across school years. The systems-ecological perspective accounts for the student's opportunity to learn at school and outside of school, and focuses the assessment-intervention link on how educators and parents can support the student to meet the task demands at school.

What is FAAB?

FAAB is a system to: (a) gather information relevant to a referral concern for an individual student, (b) assess the instructional needs for the student, (c) assess supportive learning conditions, and (d) assist educators in designing feasible instructional interventions. Teachers refer students for genuine reasons. Teachers refer a student for intervention assistance because they

want a change in the classroom, a change for the student and other students. When teachers refer a student to the intervention assistance (e.g., prereferral) team, it reflects their belief that the student can perform better and a change in the student's environment can influence his/her academic behavior and performance. *FAAB* helps professionals answer the question, "What can be done by educators/and/or parents to improve this student's school performance?" To paraphrase Tyler (1950), the question becomes, "What can be done to intentionally manipulate the classroom or home environment to foster a more appropriate response from the student?" *FAAB* allows professionals to analyze conditions in the target student's classroom, home, and home-school relationship that can be altered. It allows professionals a chance to analyze antecedent conditions with respect to the student's current academic behavior. It allows professionals to capture a picture of the affordances in the student's environment (or supports) for the student to make a more successful adaptation to task demands.

FAAB is not to be used to evaluate or say what is wrong with the student, the classroom task, the teacher's instructional strategy, home support for learning, or the family-school relationship. It is designed to identify ways to change learning environments so that the student is responding to instruction more positively and to enhance a student's academic competence.

FAAB provides a checklist of alterable variables associated with positive academic performance. These variables represent different learning conditions (what helps structure and supports learning for individual students). Specifically, variables are delineated in three categories: instructional support for learning, home support for learning, and home-school support for learning. As a result, referrals become an educational issue that requires the attention of key stakeholders for creating conditions for enhancing student engagement and learning. A successful outcome when using *FAAB* as a structure for intervention planning would be for the target student to be making a more successful adaptation to classroom instruction.

Typically, assessment is thought of as testing the learner to identify specific strengths and weaknesses. *FAAB* requires assessing the learner in context. The student's needs are assessed in relation to specific instructional tasks and in relation to specific support for learning strategies. Assessment is conceptualized as an integral part of the assessment-intervention link. Thus, the effects of an intervention on the student are considered invaluable information. *FAAB* helps professionals determine under what conditions the student responds most optimally on school-related tasks.

Table 1 presents critical features of an assessment-intervention link. It is essential for professionals to consider the attitudes and beliefs, knowledge domains, and actions and behaviors that characterize the effective use of *FAAB*.

What are the FAAB components?

Students learn because they have high rates of academic learning time; they are engaged in academically relevant tasks with a high degree of success (Fischer & Berliner, 1985; Marliave & Filby, 1985). Although student performance depends on what students do, their performance is influenced either positively or negatively by the kinds of support they receive for learning. Support occurs at school and at home. In recognition of the fact that an ecological perspective is needed to develop an assessment-intervention link for a student, the *FAAB* components are categorized in three areas of support for students:

- **Instructional Support for Learning—** which occurs in classrooms in school.
- **Home Support for Learning—**which occurs in out-of-school hours (at home or in the community).
- **Home-School Support for Learning—** which represents the degree of continuity across home and school and the quality of the relationship for working as partners to support student learning.

FAAB consists of 23 Support for Learning components (see *Figure 3*) in three contexts: 12 classroom components, 5 home components, and 6 home-school relationship components. These components focus on how to make feasible changes to address the instructional needs for an individual student.

Definitions for the 12 Instructional Support for Learning components, which are grouped into

Table 1

CRITICAL FEATURES UNDERLYING AN ASSESSMENT-INTERVENTION LINK

Attitudes and Beliefs:

- ▶ Define student behavior in specific, observable language

- ▶ Define the purpose of assessment as developing and evaluating the effect of an intervention on student responding

- ▶ View assessment as a dynamic, ongoing process that is modified and embellished by the teaching act

Knowledge Domains:

- ▶ Know empirically-documented correlates of successful academic performance

- ▶ Understand the collaborative problem-solving process

Actions and Behaviors:

- ▶ Examine all factors (school, home, classroom, student, peer) that influence the student's response to learning

- ▶ Consider the interrelationship among student, task, and strategy characteristics (i.e., What are the student's characteristics in relation to the task demands in relation to the supportive strategy used by parents and teachers?)

- ▶ Determine how the student's behavior is influenced by different environmental inputs (e.g., How does the student respond under different instructional conditions?)

- ▶ Maintain a problem-solving orientation during which consensus is reached about the student's instructional needs and feasibility of selected interventions

- ▶ Be an instructional resource by creating a file of excellent instructional interventions and resources

FUNCTIONAL
ASSESSMENT OF
ACADEMIC
BEHAVIOR

Figure 3

SUPPORT FOR LEARNING COMPONENTS

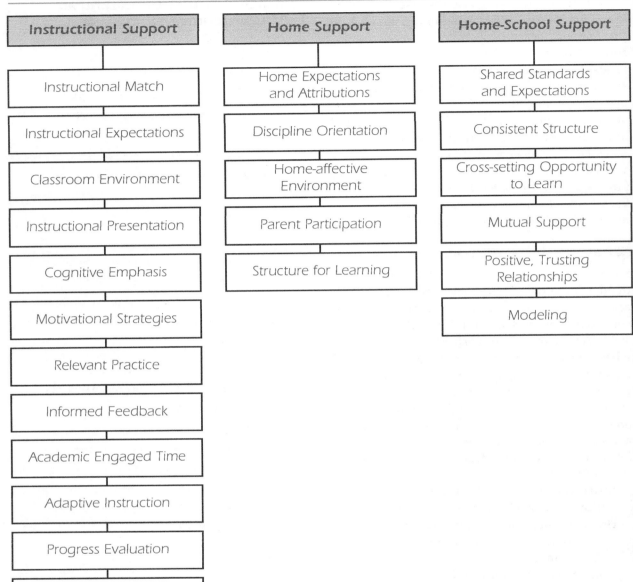

Instructional Support	Home Support	Home-School Support
Instructional Match	Home Expectations and Attributions	Shared Standards and Expectations
Instructional Expectations	Discipline Orientation	Consistent Structure
Classroom Environment	Home-affective Environment	Cross-setting Opportunity to Learn
Instructional Presentation	Parent Participation	Mutual Support
Cognitive Emphasis	Structure for Learning	Positive, Trusting Relationships
Motivational Strategies		Modeling
Relevant Practice		
Informed Feedback		
Academic Engaged Time		
Adaptive Instruction		
Progress Evaluation		
Student Understanding		

four areas (planning, managing, delivering, and evaluating instruction), appear in *Table 2*. The four areas are those identified by Algozzine and Ysseldyke (1992) as part of the Algozzine-Ysseldyke Model of Effective Instruction.

Definitions for the 5 Home Support for Learning components appear in *Table 3*. We know

that: (a) home environmental influences are positive correlates of students' academic achievement and school performance; (b) parent involvement in schooling is positively associated with the kind of student benefits desired by educators (e.g., improvement in grades, attitude toward schoolwork, behavior, self-esteem, completion of

Table 2

INSTRUCTIONAL SUPPORT FOR LEARNING COMPONENTS FOR FAAB

Instructional Planning: Decisions are made about what to teach and how to teach the student. Realistic expectations are communicated to the student.

▶ **Instructional Match:** The student's needs are assessed accurately, and instruction is matched appropriately to the results of the instructional diagnosis.

▶ **Instructional Expectations:** There are realistic, yet high, expectations for both the amount and accuracy of work to be completed by the student, and these are communicated clearly to the student.

Instructional Managing: Effective instruction requires managing the complex mix of instructional tasks and student behaviors that are part of every classroom interaction. This means making decisions that control and support the orderly flow of instruction. To do this, teachers make decisions about classroom rules and procedures, as well as how to handle disruptions, how to organize classroom time and space to be most productive, and how to keep classrooms warm, positive, and accepting places for the student with different learning preferences and performances.

▶ **Classroom Environment:** The classroom management techniques used are effective for the student; there is a positive, supportive classroom atmosphere; and, time is used productively.

Instructional Delivering: Decisions are made about how to present information, as well as how to monitor and adjust presentations to accommodate individual differences and enhance the learning of the student.

▶ **Instructional Presentation:** Instruction is presented in a clear and effective manner; the directions contain sufficient information for the student to understand the kinds of behaviors or skills that are to be demonstrated; and, the student's understanding is checked.

▶ **Cognitive Emphasis:** Thinking skills and learning strategies for completing assignments are communicated explicitly to the student.

▶ **Motivational Strategies:** Effective strategies for heightening student interest and effort are used with the student.

▶ **Relevant Practice:** The student is given adequate opportunity to practice with appropriate materials and a high success rate. Classroom tasks are clearly important to achieving instructional goals.

▶ **Informed Feedback:** The student receives relatively immediate and specific information on his/her performance or behavior; when the student makes mistakes, correction is provided.

Instructional Evaluating: Effective instruction requires evaluating. Some evaluation activities occur during the process of instruction (i.e., when teachers gather data during instruction and use those data to make instructional decisions). Other evaluation activities occur at the end of instruction (e.g., when the teacher administers a test to determine whether a student has met instructional goals).

▶ **Academic Engaged Time:** The student is actively engaged in responding to academic content; the teacher monitors the extent to which the student is actively engaged and redirects the student when the student is unengaged.

▶ **Adaptive Instruction:** The curriculum is modified within reason to accommodate the student's unique and specific instructional needs.

▶ **Progress Evaluation:** There is direct, frequent measurement of the student's progress toward completion of instructional objectives; data on the student's performance and progress are used to plan future instruction.

▶ **Student Understanding:** The student demonstrates an accurate understanding of what is to be done and how it is to be done in the classroom.

FUNCTIONAL
ASSESSMENT OF
ACADEMIC
BEHAVIOR

Table 3

HOME SUPPORT FOR LEARNING COMPONENTS FOR FAAB

▶ **Home Expectations and Attributions:** High, realistic expectations about schoolwork are communicated to the child, and the value of effort and working hard in school is emphasized.

▶ **Discipline Orientation:** There is an authoritative, not permissive nor authoritarian, approach to discipline, and the child is monitored and supervised by the parents.

▶ **Home-affective Environment:** The parent-child relationship is characterized by a healthy connectedness; it is generally positive and supportive.

▶ **Parent Participation:** There is an educative home environment, and others participate in the child's schooling and learning, at home and/or at school.

▶ **Structure for Learning:** Organization and daily routines facilitate the completion of schoolwork and support for the child's academic learning.

homework, attendance, academic perseverance, participation in classroom learning activities, greater enrollment in post secondary education, lower dropout rates, realization of exceptional talents); and (c) the specific actions families take to facilitate their children's educational success is more important for academic progress than who the students are (Christenson & Sheridan, 2001). Social class or family configuration predicts up to 25% of variance in achievement, whereas family support for learning or interaction style, referred to as the curriculum of the home, predicts up to 60% of variance in achievement (Walberg, 1984).

In *Table 4*, definitions for the 6 Home-School Support for Learning components are provided. Viewing student performance from a school and home perspective is relevant because we know: (a) the power of out-of-school time, which includes community and peer influences for school learning, is influential; (b) programs that improve student performance are comprehensive, well planned, and provide options for family involvement, which allows schools to be responsive to family diversity; and (c) the degree of match

between home and school contexts is a contributing factor for students' school success (Christenson & Sheridan, 2001).

Hansen (1986) demonstrated achievement gains from third to fifth grades for those students who experienced congruence in rules and interaction styles across home and school environments. He also found that the greater the discontinuity between home and school, the more students' academic grades declined. Also, gains in student performance are greater when a coordinated system intervention (home and school), in contrast to

Table 4

HOME-SCHOOL SUPPORT FOR LEARNING COMPONENTS FOR FAAB

▶ **Shared Standards and Expectations:** The level of expected performance held by key adults for the student is congruent across home and school, and reflects a belief that the student can learn.

▶ **Consistent Structure:** The overall routine and monitoring provided by key adults for the student have been discussed and are congruent across home and school.

▶ **Cross-setting Opportunity to Learn:** The variety of learning options available to the youth during school hours and outside of school time (i.e., home and community) supports the student's learning.

▶ **Mutual Support:** The guidance provided by, the communication between, and the interest shown by adults to facilitate student progress in school is effective. It is what adults do on an ongoing basis to help the student learn and achieve.

▶ **Positive, Trusting Relationships:** The amount of warmth and friendliness; praise and recognition; and the degree to which the adult-youth relationship is positive and respectful. It includes how adults in the home, in the school, and in the community work together to help the student be a learner.

▶ **Modeling:** Parents and teachers demonstrate desired behaviors and commitment and value toward learning and working hard in their daily lives to the student.

FUNCTIONAL
ASSESSMENT OF
ACADEMIC
BEHAVIOR

a singular system intervention (classroom or parent only), is used. There is evidence that performance for preschoolers is best when family interventions in addition to child interventions are implemented (Ramey & Ramey, 1998). Similarly, Heller and Fantuzzo (1993) demonstrated that fourth- and fifth-grade African-American students who receive reciprocal peer tutoring (RPT) and parent involvement (PI) evidenced greater math gains than similar students who received only RPT. Based on teacher ratings, students in the RPT and PI group demonstrated better work habits, higher level of motivation, more task orientation, less disruptive behavior, and were more interpersonally confident than those in the RPT only group.

Research on conjoint behavioral consultation has found that interactions involving parents, teachers, and school psychologists in joint problem solving are effective with academic, social, and behavioral concerns (Sheridan, 1997). Sheridan, Kratochwill, and Elliott (1990) found that when parents were involved actively in consultation-based problem solving, students' demonstration of important social skills were greater and longer-term than when consultative problem solving occurred in the school setting only. Likewise, Galloway and Sheridan (1995) reported a study wherein students with inconsistent academic performance responded more favorably and more consistently when conjoint (i.e., parent and teacher) problem solving occurred, as compared to conditions when parents were only peripherally involved (i.e., told what to do by school personnel).

Christenson and Christenson (1998) reviewed over 200 studies that examined the relationship between family, school, or community influences and positive school performance for students in grades K-12. A variety of dependent variables surfaced and included performance on standardized tests, grades, teacher ratings of academic performance, and measures of school adjustment, including improved attendance, fewer suspensions, increased classroom participation, and improved self-esteem and motivation to learn. Remarkable similarity in the contextual influences that enhanced student learning emerged as a result of examining studies from family, school, and community literature simultaneously. Correlations between family, school, or community influences and indicators of positive school performance

were significant and fell within the low (.10) to strong (.80) range; however, most were in the low moderate to moderate range. Actually, the size of the correlation has been argued to be less important than the fact that findings are consistent and point in a similar direction, suggesting convergence in the factors critical for students' school success (Brophy & Good, 1986; Christenson, Rounds, & Gorney, 1992). They concluded there is evidence for a common set of contextual influences important for learning regardless of the child's immediate home or school setting. Specifically, students perform most optimally when they experience six factors in school (from teachers) and outside of school (from parents and their community): standards and expectations, structure, opportunity to learn, support, climate/relationships, and modeling. These factors represent the home-school support for learning factors in *FAAB*.

Assumptions About the Components

We have made several assumptions about the support for learning components within and across the three categories. The assumptions are listed in *Table 5*. First, we recognize that the components are not necessarily mutually exclusive. Nor are the components within these three areas ranked in order of importance. Members of the intervention planning team or those involved in the consultation collaboratively decide on the components that represent the highest priority need for the target student. We have assumed that careful, systematic gathering of data about the student's learning context will allow for accurate or relevant clinical judgment about the student's highest priority needs.

Second, the use of time for and by the student is a critical factor in assessing a student's instructional needs in context. Asking: "What has been (and is) the student's opportunity to learn this material?" helps maintain a focus on availability of supports for learning in general and for skills (assigned tasks) in particular. We know from our literature review that a student's time in and out of school is a critical factor for student performance in school. Time is constant and levels the playing field in that everyone has 24 hours per day. However, how time is used for students, especially for those students who need additional time to learn, is often a variable that differentiates higher and lower achievers in classrooms. We have

FUNCTIONAL
ASSESSMENT OF
ACADEMIC
BEHAVIOR

Table 5

ASSUMPTIONS UNDERLYING THE FAAB COMPONENTS

- ▶ They are not mutually exclusive.
- ▶ They are not ranked in order of importance.
- ▶ They represent alterable variables.
- ▶ Student use of time is an alterable variable.
- ▶ When parents and educators work as partners to influence the student's opportunity to learn, the student's performance will be optimal.
- ▶ All students can learn and make daily progress when positive learning conditions are present.
- ▶ Rate of student learning progress depends on student characteristics **and** use of appropriate learning supportive strategies in school and home contexts.
- ▶ Systematic gathering of data about the student's total learning environment enhances the accuracy of clinical judgment.
- ▶ Clinical judgment of skilled professionals is essential in determining the student's instructional needs.
- ▶ Evaluation of the student's response when an intervention has been implemented affirms or disconfirms clinical judgment.

ance. We have assumed that by emphasizing protective factors or alterable conditions associated with positive indicators of academic performance, the target student would demonstrate improvement and progress. Throughout assessment and intervention planning we encourage individuals to maintain a focus on the individual student. To this end, three questions are helpful:

1. What does the student need to be successful on the task?
2. What needs to be manipulated to produce a better student response?
3. What resources do teachers and parents desire to assist the student?

These questions help guide professionals to identify supports that reliably predict or maintain positive academic behavior for a student.

THE "WHY" OF FAAB

Five reasons stand out as critically important for why an assessment of contextual supports for learning is important for improving academic behavior. These reasons, which appear in *Table 6*, explain the rationale for understanding a student's instructional need in their total learning environment.

assumed that time is alterable and parents and educators can intentionally manipulate how time is used.

Third, our focus is on alterable environmental factors (i.e., supports) that can enhance a student's academic competence. These supports are consistent with the notion of protective factors within a resilience framework. Although we recognize that differential student performance in school is a reality, we believe all students need to and can make daily progress. All students can be engaged learners and make progress; however, they won't all achieve at the same levels. Their rate of progress depends on the interaction with key stakeholders and ongoing presence of specific influences in their total learning environment. The focus of intervention must be on what can be done by parents and teachers to improve the target student's perform-

Table 6

REASONS FOR ASSESSING INSTRUCTIONAL ENVIRONMENTS

- ▶ Importance of opportunity to learn explanations for student progress and performance
- ▶ Many factors influence student outcomes
- ▶ Learning does not occur in a vacuum
- ▶ There are limits to what is learned by only assessing the learner
- ▶ Instructional Relevance: Creating an assessment to intervention link

Reason one: Importance of opportunity to learn explanations for student progress and performance

Traditional assessment practices focus on describing student characteristics, often thought of as within-student explanations (e.g., mental retardation, visual sequential memory disorder) for poor school performance. Much data are generated about what the student knows at one point in time and the student's standing relative to age or grade peers. Opportunity to learn explanations for the student must also be considered, and an identification of what type of support the student needs to be a learner is integral to effective intervention planning. Gathering data on how the student performs under different learning conditions provides relevant information about protective factors that facilitate best student performance. Enhancing the student's opportunity to learn over time is a goal of *FAAB*. The quality, intensity, and frequency of supportive learning strategies must be considered.

Reason two: Many factors influence student outcomes

There are many reasons why students perform well in school or less well than desired. The degree of learning for an individual student is a function of both student and instructional support factors. Learning problems can be conceptualized as a discrepancy between student performance and/or needs and the task demands (either too low or too high) in the environment. Educators and families help students meet environmental demands when they provide structure and support sensitive to students' specific needs.

School, home, teacher, and instructional factors are significantly and moderately correlated with positive learning outcomes for students with and without disabilities (Christenson, 2000; Christenson & Buerkle, 1999; Christenson & Christenson, 1998; Christenson et al., 1992; Henderson & Berla, 1994; Ysseldyke & Christenson, 1987, 1993). Thus, neither teachers nor families determine students' level of school performance; however, they can facilitate or inhibit optimal student performance. Examples of empirically documented ways in which teachers and families encourage students' success in school appear in *Table 7*.

Table 7

EXAMPLES OF TEACHERS AND FAMILIES AS FACILITATORS OF STUDENT LEARNING

Families	Teachers
► Encouraging and discussing leisure reading	► Matching instruction to the student's level of skill development
► Monitoring and joint analysis of television viewing	► Communicating realistic expectations to the student
► Showing interest in children's academic and personal growth	► Modifying instruction by using alternative instructional options and by using differing levels of pace to meet the needs of individual students
► Engaging in frequent dialogue with children	► Taking opportunities to praise students for good work
► Encouraging children's academic pursuits	► Keeping students actively engaged in instruction
► Setting clear and consistent limits	► Setting clear and consistent rules
► Monitoring consistently how time is spent	► Telling students it is OK to make mistakes, but be sure to learn from them
► Communicating regularly with school personnel	► Communicating regularly with parents or caregivers
► Attending and participating in school functions	► Modeling correct performance of tasks and assignments
► Displaying parental warmth and nurturance toward the child	► Displaying teacher warmth and nurturance making sure that school is a positive experience for the student
► Providing quality reading materials and math experiences	► Providing students with many opportunities for success
► Modeling learning by reading and using math in daily life	► Having students correct their work
► Reading with children	► Keeping records of student progress or teaching students to chart their own progress
► Believing children's effort, not luck, will result in learning	► Regularly informing students of their performance and progress
► Orienting a child's attention to learning opportunities	► Modeling thinking skills

FUNCTIONAL
ASSESSMENT OF
ACADEMIC
BEHAVIOR

Carroll's (1963) model of school learning, which is presented in *Figure 4*, is relevant to *FAAB* in that it states parameters of learning for students with different characteristics under different instructional conditions. According to Carroll, the amount a student learns is a function of the time the student actually spends learning divided by the amount of time the student needs to learn. The amount of time spent learning is influenced by opportunity and perseverance, particularly when the task becomes more difficult and the student may be facing failure. The time needed to learn is dependent on the student's aptitude, ability to understand instruction, and quality of instruction.

There is interconnectedness among the three determinants of time needed to learn. If the quality of instruction is less than optimal for the individual student, he or she may be disadvantaged by instruction that does not provide a good person-environment fit. The extent of this barrier is influenced by the student's ability to understand instruction. Students with a high ability to understand will be able to overcome difficulties created by a mismatch in instruction for them. However, students who require additional instructional supports to be engaged and successful on a task will be challenged to the point that their perseverance and motivation to learn will be reduced. It is noteworthy for intervention planning that four of the five variables in Carroll's model can be considered alterable; only student aptitude would be classified as a fixed variable. And, if the student's aptitude is lower, the other variables, according to Carroll, take on much greater significance for success in mainstream classrooms. It is well supported that high achieving students can perform adequately with more implicit instruction; however, low achieving students perform best with explicit, teacher-directed instruction (Chall, 2000).

Similarly, students experience differential support for learning in their home environments. According to Sloane (1991), "It is now well accepted that the home plays an important role in children's learning and achievement. Some children learn values, attitudes, skills, and behaviors in the home that prepare them well for the tasks of school (p. 161)." What is now clear is that factors in home and school environments influence the academic behavior of students, and that it is the interaction of learner characteristics with home and school supports for learning that must be understood.

Reason three: Learning does not occur in a vacuum

Students' learning problems are functionally related to the setting in which they occur. This does not mean classrooms or homes cause learning problems; however, it suggests that learning problems are triggered or influenced by instructional factors in the classroom and school environment, the degree to which the home is supportive of school learning, and the degree to which the home-school relationship is collaborative. The goal of *FAAB* is to conduct a functional assessment of ways to enhance a student's academic behavior.

We know that student, teacher, classroom, school district, and home characteristics interact to influence academic outcomes. The theoretical basis for assessing supports for learning (i.e., instructional environment) comes from Bandura's (1978)

Figure 4

CARROLL'S MODEL OF SCHOOL LEARNING

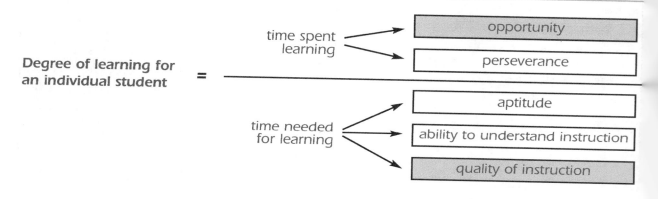

concept of reciprocal determinism. Bandura theorized that behavior is determined by a continuous reciprocal interaction among behavioral, cognitive, and environmental influences. Thus, student performance in the classroom is a function of student characteristics interacting with the nature of instructional tasks and with what teachers do instructionally. Similarly, student behavior at home is a function of student characteristics interacting with the nature of home tasks and with what parents do to support learning. Extended to the coordinated system of home and school (Bronfenbrenner, 1979), it is critical to remember that the home is influenced by what occurs at school and school is influenced by what occurs at home. The home-school relationship is yet another source of variation in children's learning. From our point of view, a good academic support plan has a good contextual fit if the interventions work well in the target environment (school, home, and home-school) and resources are available for individuals to implement the intervention.

Reason four: There are limits to what is learned by only assessing the learner

Assessing a student's learning needs in context does not serve as a substitute for norm-referenced standardized testing. Both approaches are important, depending upon the question to be addressed. Limited information is obtained from standardized tests for developing educational strategies. Other shortcomings of using only standardized tests in intervention planning are their limited relationship to actual classroom activities, i.e., the fact that testing observations (e.g., one-to-one) differ from the student's classroom performance and behavior, and that reasons for students receiving the same score on standardized tests are different (Howell, 1986). Classroom teachers have articulated the limits of standardized testing when they have noted that the test results do not apply to their situation or little information has been generated to tell them how to best help each student perform. Teachers want instructionally relevant information when they express

concerns about students' learning and performance.

Reason five: Instructional relevance: Creating an assessment to intervention link

Teachers and parents desire instructionally relevant information. They want to know what helps a student learn best. *FAAB* provides a framework to engage in collaborative intervention planning with teachers and across home and school. It does not tell educators which exact instructional strategy to use, but instead provides a systematic way for educators to gather information on critical support for learning variables associated with higher achievement in schools. It is a system for fusing theory and practice.

The *FAAB* framework focuses language among school personnel and between families and educators on factors that have been shown to be associated with positive academic behavior and performance. In this sense, communication is more solution-oriented; namely, there is a focus on what is worth trying and evaluating to examine improved progress for the target student. Also, the 23 components provide educators and families a shared language for discussing a student's instructional needs. Instructional Support for Learning (in classrooms) can be discussed in terms of supports and/or feasible changes in the areas of planning, managing, delivering, and evaluating instruction for the student, while the Home Support for Learning can be discussed in terms of parents selecting how they want to support their child's school performance. Both parents and educators can assess whether they are fairly congruent in the messages they are giving to the target student with the Home-School Support for Learning components. The focus is always on the question: "What can parents and teachers do differently and together to better support the student's learning and progress?" Functional analysis allows the individual to identify the relationship between environmental supports and the academic behavior of the student by testing hypothesis about the occurrence or nonoccurrence of the student's academic behavior and the presence of environmental supports associated with the behavior. Evaluation of the degree to which the instructional changes in the student's total learning environment improve student performance must occur. We can generate hypothesis about "what works" for a student, but until the intervention has been tried and evaluated, the relationship between the environmental supports and occurrence of positive academic behavior for the student remains undocumented. Obtaining high ratings of parent and teacher satisfaction is also critical to have a good contextual fit.

Intervention acceptability by parents and teachers is as important as intervention impact on the student's performance, largely because of issues related to intervention integrity or fidelity of implementation. If parents and teachers do not believe the intervention will make a difference for the student's learning or if either finds it not feasible to implement the intervention systematically, the likelihood that there will be sufficient follow through to impact the student's academic performance is very low. These contextual influences must be attended to during the intervention planning phase (see Chapter 3).

THE "WHEN AND WHERE" OF FAAB

When is FAAB used?

From our perspective, *FAAB* is best used proactively and preventively. As such, it will be particularly helpful to pre-referral or intervention assistance teams and in individual parent-teacher consultations about a student's academic performance. We believe that it is useful immediately when a student is having difficulty learning. This can occur when a teacher has a concern and wants to develop an intervention for the student. It will also be useful for discussing with parents the student's particular instructional needs and requesting parent support for student learning. Although parents are interested in the overall educational performance of students in schools across the nation, they are overwhelmingly most interested in how their children perform. Parents are most interested and involved when school personnel address their child's needs; parents want a personal touch and

desire information about how to help their child learn (Christenson & Sheridan, 2001).

FAAB provides a framework for understanding the ecological perspective related to children's success in school. It helps educators integrate the comprehensive literature on factors associated with varied indicators of positive school performance (e.g., tests, teacher ratings of academic competence, greater classroom participation, higher rates of task completion, better attendance, and fewer behavioral referrals). School personnel who are involved in developing family-school partnership programs to enhance school experiences and educational outcomes for children and youth will find *FAAB* a beneficial resource related to factors that enhance student learning across home and school contexts.

FAAB can be used to create an assessment-intervention link. Thus, it is applicable when referral questions include: "What does the student need to be successful in the classroom or on specific tasks? What instructional supports need to be in place to enhance student's progress? How can parents and teachers support student learning?"

Where is FAAB used?

FAAB can be used in any classroom setting whether a general or special education classroom, a larger or smaller classroom. It is used when the questions asked about the target student are a variation of "How can we as educators and parents create the most optimal conditions for this student's learning?" or "Under what conditions or with what kinds of instructional supports for learning does the target student perform most optimally?" Special education or Title I classrooms are placements, not interventions. *FAAB* is useful when individuals want to improve the learning conditions, as reflected by the student's response to instruction, for an individual student. In all cases, the intervention designed must be feasible.

CHAPTER 2

How to Use FAAB

In this chapter we identify and describe nine steps in using *FAAB*. The steps move from initial clarification of the referral concern raised by a classroom teacher or parent through data collection, prioritizing and planning interventions, implementing the interventions, and evaluating their effectiveness. The steps we list and describe are those involved in carrying out both an assessment of the instructional environment and a set of interventions based on that assessment. The overall objective of this process is the identification of instructional needs and the design of effective instructional interventions to meet those needs. The set of steps we identify match nicely with major consultation models (Sheridan, Kratochwill, & Bergan, 1996; Zins & Kratochwill, 1993), functional assessment and intervention, and the Iowa Problem Solving Model (Reschly, Tilley, & Grimes, 2000). These consultation, intervention, and problem-solving models include several steps: problem clarification, generation of alternative hypotheses about how to solve the problem, implementation of one or more alternative treatments or interventions, monitoring of success, and evaluation of the effectiveness of the treatment or intervention. *FAAB*'s nine steps are shown in *Table 8*.

Table 8

THE STEPS IN USING FAAB

1. Identify and Clarify the Referral Concern
2. Understand the Student's Instructional Needs From the Perspective of the Teacher and the Parents
3. Collect Data on the Student's Instructional Environment
4. Prioritize and Plan Interventions to Meet the Student's Instructional Needs
5. Identify Ways for Home Support for Learning
6. Implement the Intervention
7. Evaluate the Effectiveness of the Instructional Intervention
8. Revise the Intervention Plan
9. Document the Intervention and Report Results

THE STEPS

Step One: Identify and Clarify the Referral Concern

Referral is a process in which a teacher or parent says that, "A student is doing or not doing something, it bothers me, and someone should do something about the referral concern or I am going to get increasingly frustrated." Indeed, when teachers or parents refer students they are frustrated. It is typically the case that they have tried a number of alternative ways of dealing with a problem or concern and have met with limited success. It is also true that teachers refer students because they are concerned. They want the student to perform better, and they recognize that without supplemental support the probability is low that this will occur. The first step in intervention planning is to identify and clarify the teacher's and/or parent's concerns. One way to do so is to have the teacher or parent list the areas of concern and then rank these. The top two or three concerns should then be the focus of the intervention. Examples of concerns are as follows:

1. The student makes many errors in oral reading.
2. The student reads passages, but answers comprehension questions with about 50% accuracy.
3. The student has difficulty staying engaged in tasks.

The referring teacher should be asked to state the actual level and the desired level of performance for the student. Specific, observable, and measurable language should be used. The goal of the planning team is to design an intervention to help close the discrepancy (gap) between actual (i.e., problematic) and desired (i.e., acceptable) performance in the classroom. Teams should take into account discrepancies between observed and desired competencies, specify interventions that are to be implemented, and track the effectiveness of the implementation.

Teams or individuals should use the *Intervention Documentation Record* (see the Appendix at the back of the manual) to keep track of the interventions that have been implemented and their effectiveness. Information on the relative effectiveness of various interventions will be invaluable to teams as they plan subsequent interventions, especially across school years. Too often in the assessment process data on the student's instructional history is not available.

Step Two: Understand the Student's Instructional Needs from the Perspective of the Teacher and the Parents

The *Instructional Needs Checklist* (see the Appendix at the back of the manual) is used to get information about the teacher's perspective of the student's instructional needs. The *Instructional Needs Checklist* allows the consultant to gather information from the teacher about the student's strengths and weaknesses, instructional needs, and response to different tasks and materials. Teachers have a wealth of information about a student's perform-

ance and the checklist format allows for a concise way to summarize this information. Successful interventions (e.g., those for whom the teacher is committed to implementation) address the teacher's concerns. An individual teacher or a group of teachers can complete the checklist.

Designing and implementing effective interventions across school and home requires inviting parents into the assessment-to-intervention planning process early. It is important to call the parents as soon as a teacher concern arises, express the school-based concern in specific, behavioral language, and express confidence about designing a solution (especially if home and school are working together as partners). Equally important is gathering the parent's observations and experiences with the student's learning. This can be done quickly by asking the parent to name their two areas of concern for the student's school progress and two areas of strength for the student. If more detailed information is needed, the parent could respond to the questions provided in the form *Parental Experience With Their Child's Learning and Schoolwork*, which appears in the Appendix at the back of the manual. The advantage of gathering information from parents is that they can be an excellent resource, providing understanding about the student's instructional history across school years. Also, fostering this meaningful role for families in the assessment process encourages an equalitarian relationship and meaningful dialogue between home and school (Harry, 1992).

Step Three: Collect Data on the Student's Instructional Environment

Salvia and Ysseldyke (2001) indicate that there are only four ways to gather information about students: observation, recollection, review records, and test (or administer performance events). Each of these methods (their merits and limitations) will be described briefly. There is no specifically prescribed set of data collection methods that must be used in using *FAAB*. It is not always necessary to interview the student or the parent. Similarly, it is not always necessary to review student records. However, assessors should **always use at least two methods of data collection**. Decide which and how many methods are necessary to provide adequate evidence for designing an intervention.

based on the 23 Support for Learning components. Most users of *FAAB* found it necessary to observe the student in classrooms. Also, most users gathered data by interviewing teachers, parents, and students.

Observation

Observation can provide highly accurate, detailed, verifiable information about the person being observed. Data may be collected using systematic or nonsystematic procedures. When using systematic observation, the observer gathers data on one or more precisely defined skills, and the performance of the skill is recorded. Nonsystematic observation is informal observation in which the observer watches an individual and takes notes on student activities. Nonsystematic observation is anecdotal and can be subjective and difficult to replicate. Therefore, we recommend that people who use *FAAB* engage in systematic observation. The *Observation Record* form in the Appendix orients the observer to understanding student behavior in context. As can be seen on the form, the user's observations are guided by the critical question: How is the student's performance affected by_____? Thus, a goal for the observer is to describe student behavior and performance under specific conditions. Look for functional relationships as now required by the assessment provisions of the Individuals with Disabilities Education Act. That is, look carefully at the factors in the classroom or home environment that are triggering the behavior, and look at the consequences that are leading to the behavior being maintained or extinguished. The *Observation Record* form may be copied and used to guide your observations. When using the form note those things you observe about how the student responds to instructional support factors in the areas of planning, managing, delivering, and evaluating.

There are potential disadvantages in using observations to collect information: imperfect observation, time demands, and distortion of the context of observation. A substantial body of research indicates that people often imperfectly observe, interpret observations, and reach decisions based on their observations. Two types of imperfect observation are noteworthy: the halo effect and expectancy. The halo effect is the ten-

dency to make subjective judgments on the basis of general attributes (e.g., race or gender). Expectancy is the tendency to see behaviors that are consistent with one's beliefs about what should happen; the observers never would have seen these behaviors with their own eyes unless they already believed them. For example, teachers are more likely to see improved behavior on the part of their classes when they believe that their interventions are effective.

To help prevent these imperfect observations focus on making global, integative judgments. Making global, integrative judgments will be easier if one thinks of how often in the everyday world global, integrative, qualitative ratings are made. The rating criteria for *FAAB* are like evaluating a college course, rating musicians in a contest, or judging the cleanliness of a hotel room or the service of airline personnel. In each case, the criteria used to make the rating cannot be spelled out exactly. The rating is made by taking into consideration several variables, which are rated against a standard. Two examples, restaurant ratings and theatrical awards, serve to explicate the kind of rating used in *FAAB*. We hope these examples help you understand the mindset needed to make judgments about *FAAB* components.

1. *Restaurant ratings* Upon arriving in a new city, travelers depend on restaurant descriptions to select a dinner site. Many travelers consult restaurant critics. How does a restaurant receive a 5- or a 3-star rating? What is the difference between restaurants with these ratings? In granting these ratings, the critic must take many variables into consideration: the ambiance, the attentiveness of the staff, the quality of the food, the presentation of the food, the variety of food, the consistency with which the food is prepared and served, and the price.

2. *Theatrical awards* What factors are considered in presenting the "musical of the year" award? There are several. They include the content, the music, the acting, the staging, the directing, the costumes, the set design, the casting of characters, and so on.

In each of these examples, one factor does

not necessarily outweigh another in significance. When making judgments about a restaurant or musical award, all factors must be considered and integrated. The whole picture is important. For each of the *FAAB* components, we have listed a number of indicators for you to check. The greater the number of checks, the more evidence you have that the component is present in the student's instructional environment.

Recollection (through Interview, Survey, or Rating Scale)

A second important strategy for collecting data on student performance involves the use of recollection through interviews, surveys, or rating scales. Educators familiar with a student can be asked to recall observations and interpretations of performance, and can complete interviews, surveys, or rating scales based on their recollections. Data may be collected from the student (self-report or self-assessment), from teachers or other educators, and from parents. The *Student Interview Record*, in the Appendix, lists samples of the kinds of questions that students could be asked. The student interview aims to understand the student's perspective about conditions under which he/she performs better or learns more. We have also indicated sample questions that teachers might be asked. Note that the sample questions for the teacher interview focus on capturing the teacher's perception of the student's response to instruction that has occurred (i.e., the teacher's experience with the target student). The forms may be copied and used as a basis for interviews.

At this stage, school personnel may ask parents general questions or use the *Parent Interview Record* (see the Appendix at the back of the manual). The *Parent Interview Record* provides a structure for gathering information about the five components of the home environment that are associated positively with student success in school (expectations and attributions, discipline, home affective environment, parent participation, and structure for learning). The parents are asked to give their general observations about school-related behaviors and ways they prefer to help educators address the teacher's concern about

their child. In addition, they indicate ways the student's learning is typically supported at home. Parents are asked to respond in a global fashion to help reduce defensiveness or parent guilt. The tone of the interview needs to be conversational. Interviewers are encouraged to ask additional questions and to listen to the parents' needs carefully.

A face-to-face interview is preferred because one of the purposes of interviewing parents or caregivers is to build a cooperative connection between home and school in order to benefit student learning. However, often other means of data collection are necessary because of time constraints and multiple demands in individual's lives. Therefore, phone interviews and parent completion of the form as a survey could also be used.

Rating scales can be considered the most formal kind of interview. They enable data to be gathered in a structured, sequenced, and standardized way, and facilitate data aggregation. One common kind of rating scale uses a format in which the rater responds to questions or statements by indicating the extent of his/her agreement with the statement (e.g., strongly agree, agree, neutral, disagree, and strongly disagree).

One of the strengths of recollections, of course, is that they enable collection of data about situations and environments in which direct observation is difficult or impossible (i.e., past events). For some assessments, informants (including students) may be the only source of information available. A strength of rating scales is that they allow the rater to assign a numerical value to responses instead of simply indicating whether a behavior did or did not occur. A drawback to using recollection methods is that because they rely on recollection, they are based on subjective information that is tainted by memory lapses and modifications of reality. And, of course, the longer the time between the observation and recollection, the less accurate the memory of the behavior.

Record Review

A third strategy for collecting data is to compile existing information through a review of student records. There are five kinds of existing information: school cumulative records, school databases, student products, anecdotal records, and nonschool records. There are a number of limitations to relying on records to gather information about student achievement. First, it is usually necessary to go through a lot of information in order to find what is needed to answer specific assessment questions. This process can take a long time. Second, there is no control over data collected in the past. The person who recorded the information decided what was relevant to record, and often good information about the conditions under which a student demonstrated a behavior or performed a task is not available.

Tests (administer performance events)

Testing is the process of measuring student competencies, attitudes, and behaviors by presenting a challenge or problem to the student and having him/her generate a response. One way in which a test or performance event is used in assessing instructional environments is to ask students to show you their work and how they did their work. The student may be asked to complete a performance as part of a student interview. Error analysis of the student's responses to items on norm-referenced

and criterion-referenced tests can be used to identify content for this performance demonstration.

School psychologists and other members of the intervention assistance team often use environmentally-based approaches to decipher why a student is having difficulty learning specific skills or concepts. Commonly used analogue procedures for assessing academic abilities have been described in detail by Gettinger (1988) and appear in *Table 9*.

Step Four: Prioritize and Plan Interventions to Meet the Student's Instructional Needs

It often is the case that students have multiple instructional needs, yet not all of those needs are top priority. In prioritizing needs it is usually helpful to begin with the teacher's statement of concern. Any discrepancy between the teacher's perceptions and the assessor's perceptions should be identified and discussed. After the assessors have considered all of the data gathered through observation, recollection, record review, and testing, they should then review the support for learning components to identify

Table 9

TYPES OF ANALOGUE PROCEDURES FOR ASSESSING ACADEMIC ABILITIES

Procedure	*Description*
Diagnostic Teaching	Simulated instruction that evaluates effectiveness of remedial strategies and identifies conditions under which skills are acquired.
Task Analysis	Focuses on student's level of skills in relation to instructional objective by breaking down tasks into component skills and assessing mastery of these skills.
Error Analysis	Identification of item types that are consistently failed/passed and formulation of tentative hypotheses about the student's deficits/abilities
Modified Testing	Techniques to alter or expand standardized testing procedures (modality, language, time) to determine why a student erred in responding.
Curriculum-Based Assessment	Procedure for determining instructional needs on the basis of evaluating continuous performance on existing course content and curriculum.
Work Sampling	Systemic evaluation of samples of work (writing samples, tests, completed workbook pages) that reflect the student's learning problems/strengths.

Source: Gettinger, M. (1988). Analogue assessment: Evaluating academic abilities. In E.S. Shapiro & T.R. Kratochwill (Eds.), *Behavioral assessment in schools* (pp. 247-289). New York: Guilford Press.

FUNCTIONAL
ASSESSMENT OF
ACADEMIC
BEHAVIOR

areas of priority needed for the target student. Use *The Instructional Environment Checklist* (see the Appendix at the back of the manual) to select priority areas for intervention planning. Note on the checklist that users identify, based on the information available to them, the three subscales (or areas) that need to be enhanced for the student to demonstrate greater academic success.

Identifying a student's top priority needs involves considerable professional judgment. Keep in mind that the main reason for using the *Instructional Environment Checklist* is to organize thoughts/beliefs for discussion during the intervention design phase.

Once the needs have been prioritized and there is consensus about critical supports for learning for the target student, a plan should be developed on how these needs are to be addressed. Tyler (1950) described instruction as the intentional manipulation of the learning environment to facilitate an appropriate response from the student. Team members (teachers, administrators, parents, related services personnel) should discuss ways in which they can intentionally manipulate the student's learning environment to close the gap between the student's actual and desired levels of performance. In selecting an intervention, special attention should be paid to choosing approaches or ideas that the teacher **wants** to try and that are the most feasible. Because each intervention is not equally feasible to implement, we encourage the team to discuss the feasibility questions that have been described by Rogers (1983). These questions which appear in *Table 10* have been applied to school-based situations.

Step Five: Identify Ways for Home Support for Learning

Student learning occurs in school and outside of school; therefore, the home provides an essential venue for enhancing the academic performance of students. In *Table 11*

Table 10

FEASIBILITY QUESTIONS FOR ASSESSING INTERVENTIONS

Question 1
Relative advantage: Is the new idea, practice, or intervention better than what was in place before?
(If the teacher and parent perceive the suggestions as more effective than existing practices, they are more likely to implement the change.)

Question 2
Compatibility: Is it consistent with existing values, past experiences, and needs?
(If the teacher and parent view the suggestions as consistent with existing values, responsive to student, family, and teacher needs, and supportive of school goals and plans, they are more likely to support the change.)

Question 3
Complexity: Is it perceived as difficult to understand and use?
(If the teacher and parents believe implementation requirements are clear and relatively easy, they are more likely to follow through and ensure intervention integrity.)

Question 4
Trialability: Can it be tried on a limited basis?
(If the teacher or parent have the option of trying out the intervention [i.e., a pilot], implementation is more likely to begin.)

Question 5
Observability: Are the results of implementing it observable?
(If the teacher and parents can document positive change and benefits of an intervention, they are more likely to facilitate its' implementation.)

Question 6
Resource availability: What supplemental resources are available for successful implementation of the intervention plan?
(Attention should be paid to ways in which several other individuals in the student's school and the family can work together to contribute to the intervention implementation. Keep in mind that intervention planning does not mean that only the teacher must make changes.)

Questions drawn from Rogers (1983). Rationale in parenthesis are author's application to schools.

selected findings from a recent study by the Metropolitan Life Survey on the perspectives and experiences of 1,036 students in grades 7-12 on varied aspects of family-school partnerships are provided (Binns, Steinberg, & Amorosi, 1997). These statistics do not surprise social scientists or educators who often say, "I need the support of parents to really make progress with students about whom I am concerned." These statistics do, however, surprise parents, who do not realize that student performance in school is highly influenced by how students spend their time outside of school. To address the student's total learning environment, it is essential to identify the student's needs for support for learning in the home.

Use the *Instructional Environment Checklist*'s Home Support for Learning and Home-School Support for Learning components (in the Appendix at the back of the manual) as a basis for generating possible suggestions to enhance student learning outside of school hours. Parents con-

Table 11

SELECTED FINDINGS FROM THE METROPOLITAN LIFE SURVEY

▶ 25% of students who are getting grades below C report their parents are not involved.

▶ 45% of students who get class grades lower than C do not receive parental help finding time and a place to study.

▶ 50% of students who get class grades lower than C report that their parents do not help with homework.

▶ Students who get mostly A's and B's (87%) report that their parents are available to help with schoolwork, whereas 24% of students who get grades lower than C report that their parents are not available to help with schoolwork.

▶ 78% of students who receive mostly A's and B's report their parents find the time to talk with them about their school lives; only 51% of students who get grades lower than C's report this.

Drawn from Binns et al., 1997.

---

sistently report that they want to help their children learn, but do not know how to do so (Christenson & Sheridan, 2001). Families differ in their time, skills, and knowledge about how to assist their children. Therefore, generating as many ideas as possible for home support for learning gives the parents options and increases the probability that they will follow through at home. It also carries a powerful message to parents—namely that, "We want to partner and we respect your expertise about 'what works' in your home." This is also a time to establish a system for ongoing communication between home and school. Specifically, who will be the case manager for answering questions as the intervention is implemented. Because there can be surprises for parents when they begin to implement home support for learning, it is important to ask the parent(s) what resources they will find helpful when implementing what they have chosen. Friendly "touchpoint" phone calls are encouraged.

Step Six: Implement the Intervention

An important aspect of conducting functional assessments is to systematically manipulate conditions with a planned intervention and to assess the student's response to these implemented interventions. The plan should specify who is to carry out the intervention, using what resources, in what environment, and for how long. It should also include a systematic method for gathering data on the effectiveness of the approaches used to intervene with the student. In carrying out an intervention, special attention should be given to intervention (i.e., treatment) integrity (an examination of the extent to which the intervention is implemented as intended).

Step Seven: Evaluate the Effectiveness of the Instructional Intervention

It is always necessary to record data on the effectiveness of treatments or interventions. Failure to do so (1) leaves the teacher with no record of the extent to which a treatment works, and (2) removes a "paper trail" that can be used by other teachers and diagnostic personnel, and may be particularly helpful in situations where high rates of mobility are an issue. The evaluator making a record of the intervention should note duration

FUNCTIONAL
ASSESSMENT OF
ACADEMIC
BEHAVIOR

and intensity of the intervention. Ideally, a formal method (like an ABA or multiple baseline approach) should be used in documenting interventions. Procedures for doing so are specified on pages 247-259 of *Strategies and Tactics for Effective Instruction* (Algozzine, Ysseldyke, & Elliott, 1998). After this is done, the evaluator will know the extent to which the intervention implementation and withdrawal were related to behavior change. Evaluators should also collect other evidence for the effectiveness of interventions (e.g., more work completed, more academic engaged time, or better grades). We believe there should be multiple indicators of effectiveness, including products of student work, and evidence of teacher, parent, and student satisfaction with student performance and progress.

Step Eight: Revise the Intervention Plan

When an intervention results in positive behavior change (moves a student from actual toward desired levels of behavior) this should be celebrated. It is always a good idea to celebrate success. When an intervention does not work, however, it should be modified. This involves the process of hypothesis testing. The evaluator should ask him or herself several questions both during and after the intervention is completed:

► Was the intervention put in place as anticipated?
► Was the duration of the treatment long enough?
► Was the treatment intense enough?

► Should another approach be used?
► Should different materials be used?
► Was the intervention planned appropriately?
► Was instruction appropriately managed?
► Were the methodologies used to deliver instruction effective?
► Was student performance and progress appropriately evaluated?
► Was there sufficient home support for learning?
► How does the relationship between home and school influence the student's success in school?
► How can the message about student performance in school be strengthened?

Of course, the indicators under instructional, home, and home-school support for learning components on the *Instructional Environment Checklist: Annotated Version* (see the Appendix at the back of the manual) are useful in re-evaluating effectiveness.

Step Nine: Document the Intervention and Report Results

It is critical that those who intervene keep a detailed record of the results of the intervention. The *Intervention Documentation Record*, which appears in the Appendix and can be reproduced, is very useful for this purpose. It is also helpful in meeting the assessment and reporting requirements of the 1997 revision of the Individuals with Disabilities Education Act.

CHAPTER 3

Using FAAB Results to Plan Interventions

This chapter provides examples of interventions, but it is important to point out some fundamental principles that served as a foundation for doing so. We believe:

▸ We can offer intervention ideas. Yet, professionals who have first-hand knowledge of student behavior and performance are in the best position to be creative in developing instructional interventions. These should be based on their careful analysis of the context and consensus about the support for learning factors that need to be enhanced for the individual student.

▸ Educational professionals working directly with the student are in the best position to make judgments about the quality, intensity, and frequency of interventions to achieve greater academic success for the student (i.e., a good person-environment fit for the referred student).

▸ Careful, studied analysis and sharing of information paired with problem solving among those people who have the most stake in what is done (teachers, parents, etc.) will enable the team to readily identify the starting point for interventions. As our colleagues have told us, "the problem will stare you in the face."

▸ We can offer sample interventions; however, there is danger in doing so. We do not want to stifle team creativity. A list of interventions seems highly prescriptive. We know that the interventions we list will work, but they will not **always** work for **all** students. In keeping with the principles underlying functional assessment, decisions about what works are best made by involving all key stakeholders in careful study of the student's needs in context. And, interventions must be documented and evaluated. You will only know what works for individual students by implementing and evaluating the effectiveness of interventions.

This chapter contains interventions designed to enhance its three sections: (1) Instructional Support for Learning, (2) Home Support for Learning, and (3) Home-School Support for Learning. In each section examples of interventions that can be used to enhance each of the components are listed. A list of resources to consult for a more in-depth and extensive set of strategies, tactics, and tools can be found at the end of the manual.

INSTRUCTIONAL SUPPORT FOR LEARNING

Interventions for instructional support for learning are designed to enhance application of effective instruction in each of the 12 Instructional Support for Learning components. As we have noted, instructional support includes effective planning, managing, delivering, and evaluating of instruction for individual learners. The following interventions may be applied when the assessment indicates a need for intervention in one of the 12 instructional components.

Instructional Match

The student's needs are assessed accurately and instruction is matched appropriately to the results of the instructional diagnosis.

▶ *Implement Remedial Interventions*- Provide the student with the skills necessary to be successful in instruction. Remedy skill deficits or deficiencies.

▶ *Provide Compensatory Instruction*- Design instruction to compensate for or accommodate skill deficits.

▶ *Engage in a Systematic Assessment of Skill Deficiencies*- Use norm-referenced tests, curriculum-based measures, pre-test skills, conduct environmental inventories, or use portfolios to assess student skills. Salvia and Ysseldyke (2001) provide a helpful

description of the kinds of behaviors sampled by different academic achievement tests.

▶ *Use Informal Assessment Frequently*- Informal assessment should occur frequently, be direct, and be designed to evaluate precisely what students need to learn or have been learning. In conducting an informal assessment, one should use the work students are completing on a daily basis, or the work the teacher expects them to complete in the near future. By using several levels of reading books, for example, instructional personnel should be able to identify an individual student's instructional, frustration, and independent level (Algozzine, Ysseldyke, & Elliot, 1998).

▶ *Modify Instruction for Students Who Need it*- You may need to enrich or expand learning activities for some students, while extending learning opportunities for others. It may be as simple as giving an individual student extra opportunity to practice. Or, adaptation may involve shifting, for example, from a computer to a lecture when delivering instruction (Algozzine, et al., 1998).

▶ *Examine the Relationship Between the Proficiency Level Demanded by Instructional Tasks and the Student's Level of Proficiency*- Base instruction on Howell, Fox, and Morehead's (1993) three levels of proficiency (Accuracy, Mastery, and Automaticity) as listed in *Table 12*. Doing so will involve

Table 12

LEVELS OF PROFICIENCY*

	Accuracy	*Mastery*	*Automaticity*
Definition	Identifies or produces information accurately at a preset percentage level	Identifies or produces information accurately and quickly at a preset rate.	Identifies or produces information accurately and quickly in context and/or different settings.
Content of Instruction	Example: Produce the correct quotients to division problems 100% of the time.	Example: Produce the correct answer to multiplication facts at a rate of 75 digits per minute.	Example: Produce the correct answers to addition facts completed in a checkbook.

*Student behaviors usually fall into two domains: "identify" or "produce."
Adapted from: Howell, Fox, & Morehead (1993).

helping students acquire skills and practice them to fluency (to the point that they are able to demonstrate the skills independently and automatically).

► *Deconstruct Tasks-* Conduct a task analysis to achieve a match for student skill level.

Instructional Expectations

There are realistic, yet high expectations for both the amount and accuracy of work to be completed by the student, and these are communicated clearly to the student.

► *Review the Learning Goal of the Lesson-* Sometimes goals are too high or too low.

► *Review Expectations for Class Behavior and Task Completion-* Sometimes expectations are set too high or the student is expected to complete more work than he or she is capable of. In such instances expectations should be adjusted to the point at which the student is able to complete the work with a success rate of at least 80%.

► *Ask the Student to State the Goals of the Lesson-* This enables professionals to check student understanding of expectations, and gets students actively involved.

► *Vary Question Format-* When teaching facts, for example, the teacher would encourage rapid responses to questions. When teaching concepts the teacher would give lots of examples and nonexamples for each concept. Questions would be used to elicit student examples of things that are always, sometimes, and never instances of the concept. When teaching strategies, the teacher would ask the student to show how to solve a problem in a step-by-step way.

► *Demonstrate High Expectations in the Classroom-* Call on students randomly and expect them to respond.

► *Use Peer-Mediated Learning Procedures-* Some investigators suggest assigning same-age peers, while others suggest cross-age tutoring in which older students assist younger ones. A good resource to use in implementing peer-mediated learning is *Together We Can: Classwide Peer Tutoring to Improve Basic Academic Skills* (Greenwood, Delquadri & Carta, 1997).

► *Use Contingency Contracting-* In the *Tough Kid Book*, Rhodes, Jensen, and Reavis (1996) provide lots of examples of contingency contracts.

► *Review Expectations-* Review expectations for task completion, neatness, and accuracy. Write out the expectations for specific assignments, review them with the student before he/she begins a task, review them as the student is completing the task, and again when the student has completed the task.

► *Call on the Student During Class-* Use cues and prompts to ensure student response.

Classroom Environment

The classroom management techniques used are effective for the student; there is a positive, supportive classroom atmosphere; and time is used productively.

► *Limit the Number of Rules to 5-7-* Each rule should be stated clearly and reviewed with students early and frequently during the year.

► *Give Students a Checklist of Rules and Routines-* Provide students with a checklist of the specific rules and routines for the class they attend. There are examples of checklists in *Timesavers for Educators* (Elliott, Algozzine, & Ysseldyke, 1997).

► *Give Examples of Rule Compliance-* Give students examples of appropriate and inappropriate rule compliance when teaching classroom rules.

► *Make Sure the Classroom is a Pleasant Place-* Classrooms can be made into friendly places by using general praise to support student learning ("Thanks for always being on time"), listening carefully and being supportive, and greeting students individually.

Instructional Presentation

Instruction is presented in a clear and effective manner; the directions contain sufficient information for the student to understand the kinds of behaviors or skills that are to be demonstrated; and, the student's understanding is checked.

▶ *Make Lessons Relevant to Student Background*- Students need to see personal meaning in the work they complete. Consider the extent to which the student has the necessary background and experiences to relate to the content of instruction. When the student does not, you could either provide remedial instruction or awareness education to acquaint the student with the necessary information. Or, you could modify the instruction so that it is clearly relevant to the student's experiential background.

▶ *Review the Skills the Student Already has and State Goals*- Prior knowledge is one of the most important variables of student learning. Effective instruction begins with a review of the skills students already have or of material they have already learned. Those skills necessary to complete new lessons should be reviewed and reinforced. State the instructional goals and the reasons why a lesson is important early.

▶ *Teach Learning Strategies*- Teach using mnemonics, pegword systems, the keyword method, etc. (Deshler, Shumaker, Bulgren, et al., 2001)

Cognitive Emphasis

Thinking skills and learning strategies for completing assignments are communicated explicitly to the student.

▶ *Give the Student a Checklist as a Guide or Have Students Create Their Own Checklists*- Help the student monitor his/her thinking processes. Students can be given a checklist to guide them through assignments. For example, checklists for writing assignments can include statements like, "Capitalize first words," "Put punctuation marks at the ends of sentences," "Write so it sounds like talking," and "Watch endings on action words."

▶ *Have Students Make Predictions About how They Will do*- Ask students to predict the number of correct responses they think they will make on an assignment. Then have them compare their actual performance with their predicted performance.

Talk to students about how they proceed through tasks, the extent to which they are accurate in their judgments of their own performance, and how they can be careful and deliberate in their work.

▶ *Use HDYKT*- Whenever the student asks a question, simply ask HDYKT (how do you know that). The student must then back up his/her answer with evidence of what, where, and how the answer was derived. This encourages students to back up their answers with supporting facts, theories, and details. It is also effective in diminishing the extent to which students blurt out answers without taking the time to think about the answer and defend it (Algozzine, Ysseldyke, & Elliott, 1997).

▶ *Directly Teach Learning Strategies*- Teach students to memorize, make associations, etc.

Motivational Strategies

Effective strategies for heightening student interest and effort are used.

▶ *Show Interest and Enthusiasm*- Enthusiasm is contagious. Students will be more motivated to learn things that instructors are enthusiastic about.

▶ *Make Students Believe They can do the Work*- Maintain a warm, supportive atmosphere, and select and use instructional activities that are known to produce student success.

▶ *Help Students Value Schoolwork*- Students are more likely to complete assigned work when they understand what is required of them, why it is required of them, and how it relates to past and future learning. Have students restate in their own words what they understand the purpose to be and how it relates to past, current, and future use (Algozzine, Ysseldyke, & Elliott, 1997).

▶ *Use Mystery Motivators*- When having students work for rewards, do not tell them ahead of time what the reward will be. You might put the name of the reward in an envelope with a large question mark on its outside. Display the envelope prominently in the classroom. In the *Tough Kid Book*, Rhodes, Jensen, and Reavis (1996) provide many examples of mystery motivators.

▶ *Set Personal Goals-* Write personalized goals for individual students.
▶ *Have Students Monitor Their Performance-* Motivation is enhanced when students monitor their performance in relation to personal goals and receive positive feedback for successful performance.
▶ *Recognize Students for Improvement and Progress-* Identify opportunities to publicly praise student attainments.
▶ *Use Lotteries-* Award students with lottery tickets for completion of assignments and hold periodic drawings for prizes.

Relevant Practice

The student is given adequate opportunity to practice with appropriate materials and achieve a high success rate. Classroom tasks are clearly important to achieving instructional goals.
▶ *Make Sure Practice is Relevant to Attaining Lesson Objectives-* Practice activities should be related to instructional goals and achieving good success.
▶ *Use Computer-Assisted Instructional Materials-* Computer-assisted instructional materials can provide interesting variations in practice materials, offer immediate feedback, and help students develop automaticity.
▶ *Provide Practice Frequently and Informally-* Informal, direct, and frequent practice means daily or weekly checks of student performances on instructionally relevant tasks. Provide daily opportunities to practice, especially when introducing a fact, concept, or strategy.
▶ *Vary Kinds of Practice (Drill or Generalization), Materials for Practices, and Length of Practice Sessions-* Students can get easily bored. Vary the kinds of materials (e.g., computer-assisted, manipulatives, textbooks) you use. Also, vary the length of practice sessions dependent on the intensity of the learning activity and the complexity of what is to be learned.

Informed Feedback

The student receives relatively immediate and specific information on his/her performance or behavior; when the student makes mistakes, correction is provided.
▶ *Give Corrective Feedback-* Let the student know that he or she did not do what was expected, and show them what to do. Vary the methods used to reteach and correct.
▶ *Minimize Explanations on Why Student Response is Wrong-* Maximize provision of instructions on how to perform tasks correctly.
▶ *Use a Buddy Checker-* Increase opportunity for frequent feedback about task accuracy by assigning students a buddy to check their work.

Academic Engaged Time

The student is actively engaged in responding to academic content; the teacher monitors the extent to which the student is actively engaged and redirects the student when the student is unengaged.
▶ *Be Personal-* Maintain eye contact and call on students by their name.
▶ *Make a List-* Brainstorm a list of ways that should be tried to increase the amount of time the student is actively engaged. Add to the list factors that are found to work with the student.
▶ *Check Instructional Match-* Check to be sure that the level of instruction is matched to the individual student's level of skill development, and adjust instruction to align these.
▶ *Ensure Students Understand Directions-* There are several ways to ensure that students understand directions. Two of the most common include simply asking them to tell you or show you what they must do. If you simply ask students **if** they understand, expect a simple "yes" or "no" response that will not give you the information you need.
▶ *Have Students Work in Teams-* Use cooperative learning or peer-assisted learning.

Adaptive Instruction

The curriculum is modified within reason to accommodate the student's unique and specific instructional needs.
▶ *Use Varied Methods and Materials-*

FUNCTIONAL
ASSESSMENT OF
ACADEMIC
BEHAVIOR

Intersperse the use of lecture, discussion, media, and materials.

▶ *Provide "Extras"-* Give students extra instruction or review.

▶ *Use Partially Completed Outlines-* Give students outlines to complete as lessons progress.

▶ *Use Organizers and Study Guides-* Provide study guides, learning outlines, alternative presentations (e.g., tape-recorded lectures), and self-monitoring cue cards as adaptations to accommodate individual student differences (Algozzine, Ysseldyke, & Elliott, 1997).

▶ *Use Technology to Teach-* Encourage students to use the Internet and other technology resources to extend information provided in classroom instructional presentation. Have them work together in groups to prepare class presentations extending a topic being studied. Have them share their information using varied instructional methods (e.g., overhead projectors, slide shows, dramatic presentations) (Algozzine, Ysseldyke, & Elliott, 1997).

▶ *Monitor the Effectiveness of Alternative Interventions-* Keep track of student progress, or have students keep track of their own progress. Use information on student progress to plan subsequent work.

Progress Evaluation

There is direct, frequent measurement of the student's progress toward completion of instructional objectives; data on the student's performance and progress are used to plan future instruction.

▶ *Monitor the Process Students use to Complete Their Work-* Ask the student to explain how he/she arrived at answers or how he/she does his/her work. Keep track of changes (especially improvements) over time.

▶ *Check Student Success Rate-* Keep track of student success rate, and try to keep it at about 80%.

▶ *Monitor Active Engagement-* Instructional outcomes are enhanced when students are actively engaged in responding to instruction. Keep track of the amount of time they are actively engaged, and work to increase

it. It is also effective to ask students to chart their own engaged time.

▶ *Have Students Chart Their Progress-* Use charts on the board for students to record their progress, and have them indicate with a plus or minus whether progress improved.

▶ *Check and Chart Student Success Rate-* A handy method to use when monitoring student understanding is simply to check their success rate. If a student is shown how to solve double-digit addition problems and gets 8 out of 20 correct, you would probably conclude that the student did not understand how to solve the problems. If, on the other hand, he/she got 18 out of 20 correct, you would reach a different conclusion.

▶ *Check and Chart Student Progress-* The professional literature includes a number of techniques for charting student progress. These include the baseline design, withdrawal (ABA or ABAB) design, reversal (ABCB) design, multiple baseline design, changing criterion design, and alternating treatment design. See *Table 13* for a brief illustration or pages 247-259 in *Strategies and Tactics for Effective Instruction* (Algozzine, Ysseldyke, & Elliott, 1997) for a complete description and illustration of these.

▶ *Use Student Checkers-* Assign a student checker for each row; have the roles for each student checker rotate; have all students checked within 10 minutes of independent seatwork time.

Student Understanding

The student demonstrates an accurate understanding of what is to be done and how it is to be done in the classroom.

▶ *Show me how you did it-* Students can be taken aside and asked to show an adult how they completed their work.

▶ *Use Lesson Reaction Cards-* At the conclusion of a lesson, ask students to write a brief reaction to the lesson by answering direct questions such as: "What did you learn today?"; "How does it relate to other

Table 13

ABA DESIGN	ABAB DESIGN
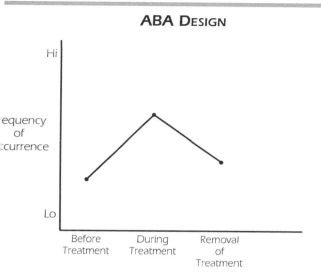	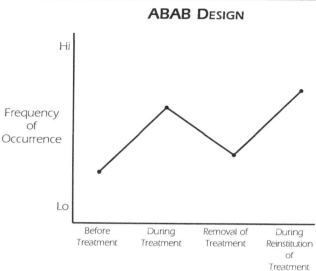

things you know?" and "What else would you like to know?"

HOME SUPPORT FOR LEARNING

Interventions for home support for learning represent the family/parental influence on the student's academic, motivational, behavioral, and social growth and performance. They are not necessarily coordinated with the instructional intervention provided by the teacher or school. Parents often want to know what they can do to assist their children's learning. School personnel who consult with parents are in an ideal position to offer suggestions to parents. It is important to allow the parent to select from several options. The goal is to determine what works for the parent. According to Walberg (1984), the "curriculum of the home predicts academic learning twice as well as the socioeconomic status of families" (p. 400) and includes these components:

► Informed parent-child conversations about everyday events
► Encouragement and discussion of leisure reading
► Monitoring and joint analysis of television viewing
► Expression of affection
► Interest in children's academic and personal growth
► Delay of immediate gratifications to accomplish long-term goals

Others (Clark, 1983; Hess & Holloway, 1984; Kellaghan, Sloane, Alvarez, & Bloom, 1993) have suggested these components:

► Strong parental encouragement of academic pursuits
► Consistent monitoring of how time is spent
► Parental responsibility for assisting children with literacy and to gain knowledge
► Parent-initiated communication with school personnel
► Helping children develop a reflective problem-solving style
► Believing children's effort, not luck or ability, will result in academic learning gains
► Fostering children's interest and skill in reading and math
► Work habits of the family emphasize a regular routine and priority for schoolwork
► Frequent encouragement of the child for his/her schoolwork
► Opportunities to explore and discuss ideas and events
► Opportunities for good language habits (i.e., effective use of language)
► Establish ambitious but realistic aspirations and expectations for the child's performance

FUNCTIONAL
ASSESSMENT OF
ACADEMIC
BEHAVIOR

Home Expectations and Attributions

High, realistic expectations about schoolwork are communicated to the children, and the value of effort and working hard in school is emphasized.

▸ *Set Realistic Expectations-* Assist parents in setting realistic expectations for their child's performance and school success by deconstructing tasks, asking parents to predict the child's success on each part, and comparing the prediction to actual child performance.

▸ *Encourage Parents to Attribute Student Success to Effort, Practice, and Hard Work-*

  ▸ Encourage parents to discuss with their child the importance and benefits of attending school and participating in school and classroom activities. (Generate phrases parents can use to recognize their child's persistence.)

  ▸ Set a specific goal and ask the parent to discuss with his/her child how the child feels as he/she makes progress toward achieving the goal.

  ▸ Ask parents to discuss with the child how learning is a process, one in which mistakes are valued because they help us to learn.

  ▸ List parental expectations for performing in school and ask the child to rate how well he/she did in meeting them.

  ▸ Encourage parents to discuss with their child the value and benefits of obtaining a good education this year. Over time parents should also discuss the value of possible career options and obtaining critical life skills.

  ▸ Encourage parents to clearly state to their child what they expect him/her to do, as well as initiating a call to teachers when a parental concern is present.

  ▸ Have parents repeat their beliefs, in an encouraging and pleasant way, about the importance of school and working hard each day.

  ▸ Encourage parents to find a regular time to discuss school-related issues with their child to ensure accountability.

  ▸ Encourage parents to ask their child about school every day. (Generate a variety of ways parents can ask about school, schoolwork, and school events.)

  ▸ Check to be sure that the goals and standards for the student's behavior are age appropriate.

  ▸ When finishing tasks, discuss effort in terms of long-term gains and short-term benefits.

  ▸ Encourage parents to recognize the child's success (includes progress and improvement) and voice expectations for continued achievement.

  ▸ Increase parents' knowledge of the student's current schoolwork, curriculum, and school activities.

  ▸ Help parents establish vocational aspirations (includes possibility for college) for their child.

Discipline Orientation

There is an authoritative (not permissive or authoritarian) approach to discipline, and the child is monitored and supervised by the parents.

▸ *Child Management and Discipline Approaches-* Discuss with parents the pros and cons of different child management and discipline approaches (permissive, authoritarian, and authoritative). Ask parents to select the disciplinary style they desire to use.

▸ *Encourage Parents to Discuss Rules and Consequences for Behavior (Appropriate and Inappropriate)-*

  ▸ Discuss a problem-solving approach to address anger management with parents such as: "Stop, think about the problem. What are your choices? Choose one. What might be the consequences of your choice? Do it. How did it work?"

  ▸ Encourage parents to negotiate clear rules and standards for age-appropriate activities.

  ▸ Encourage parents to apply sanctions appropriately and consistently.

  ▸ Encourage parents to hold regularly scheduled "touchpoint" meetings with their child to see how he/she is doing in terms of rule compliance, negotiating rules, discussing concerns, etc.

  ▸ Help parents set clear and consistent

limits for the child's behavior in terms of behavioral concerns for parents and completion of schoolwork.

▸ Ask parents about their concerns and the topics they would like more information on in order to help teach their child appropriate behavior and social skills.

▸ Devise a plan for parents to better monitor their child's use of out-of-school time (e.g., call home, request others to contact child, etc.).

Home-affective Environment

The parent-child relationship is characterized by a healthy connectedness; it is generally positive and supportive.

▸ *Ask Parents to Talk to Their Children About Their Strengths and What They do Well-*

  ▸ Ensure that the child hears the parent "bragging" about the child to others.

  ▸ Encourage the parent to spend time with his/her child. (It is particularly valuable for the parent and child to learn something new together that reflects the child's interest.)

  ▸ Encourage parents to use teachable moments (i.e., running errands as a time to talk and laugh).

  ▸ Encourage parents to ask their child about his/her point of view on a particular issue (e.g., daily event).

  ▸ Encourage parents to reward successes and notice and reward achievement, especially improvement and progress, in school. Accentuate the positive!

  ▸ Encourage parents to listen more and respond less when the child verbalizes a problem. Help parents to learn active listening skills.

  ▸ Ensure that the parent and child spend some relaxing time together on a regular basis.

  ▸ Ask parents to encourage the child to try new things and report what he/she learned.

  ▸ Encourage the parents to affirm the child's personal worth by using positive labels (e.g., pet names).

▸ Teach problem-solving structures and reflective listening skills to parents so they have a structure to deal with an emotional issue articulated by the child.

▸ Share with the parents how to set short-term and long-term goals for rewarding the child.

▸ Recognize and foster a child's special talents; consider creating a talent list to share with the school.

▸ Encourage the parents to express affection and approval and explain reasons for disapproval.

▸ Increase parental knowledge of child strengths and weaknesses so parental academic guidance and support fits the child's needs (e.g., supervision of homework may be smoother).

Parent Participation

There is an educative home environment, and others participate in the child's school and learning, at home and/or at school.

▸ *School Activities-* Encourage the parents to take part in school activities (e.g., volunteering at school, attending school functions).

▸ *Read to Children-* Encourage the parents to regularly read to children and listen to them read, as well as tell their child stories.

▸ *Communicate With Educators-* Sometimes parents do not know what to ask or share. Discuss the kinds of questions parents may want to ask and the kind of information that would be welcome by the teacher.

▸ *Open Family Discussions-* Encourage parents to arrange a time for open family discussions about the school day, parents' work and activities, and current events.

▸ *Coordinate Specific Activities-* Coordinate with the teacher so the parent has specific activities and ways to reinforce school-related tasks at home.

▸ *Reading and Discussion-* Encourage parents to provide opportunities for reading, joint viewing and analysis of television programs, and discussion of daily and world events.

▸ *Parents Role as Teacher-* Encourage parents

to enhance learning at home whether through reading, technology, visits to museums, and extracurricular activities. Help parents to see their role as "teacher" of new information to their child.

▶ *Correct Language-* Encourage parents to correct verbal language errors at home.

▶ *Use Everyday Experiences for Learning-* Discuss ways to make learning at home enjoyable. Encourage parents to use everyday experiences to teach children (e.g., household activities to reinforce school skills).

▶ *Find a Mentor-* Secure a mentor for a child whose family needs support due to excessive family demands.

Structure for Learning

Organization and daily routines facilitate the completion of schoolwork and support for the child's academic learning.

▶ *Provide Time, Space, and Materials-* Encourage parents to provide the child with time, space, and materials for studying, hobbies, and reading.

▶ *Limit Certain Activities-* Encourage parents to limit the amount of television watching, extracurricular, or work activities to ensure time for schoolwork.

▶ *Establish a Regular Routine-* Discuss and establish a regular routine for the child and family during the school week (e.g., completion of chores and good health habits, including exercise, eating, and sleep).

▶ *Arrange a Support System-* Identify who (e.g., adults, siblings) is available to support the child's learning and provide assistance with homework.

▶ *Monitor Homework Completion-* Encourage parents to monitor homework completion. Ensure that the parents have a foolproof mechanism from school for knowing about homework assignments and expectations.

▶ *Help the Parent Secure the Necessary Resources to Complete Schoolwork-* Encourage parents to consider hiring a tutor or coach, or provide them with references for a tutor.

▶ *Examine Leisure Time-* Encourage parents to examine the use of leisure time to ensure it is spent in a constructive way.

HOME-SCHOOL SUPPORT FOR LEARNING

The defining feature of home-school support for learning is that there is a coordinated intervention across home and school. Thus, both the parent/caregiver and school personnel are providing the student with a congruent message about the importance of school. Both the home and school are providing support for learning within their respective roles. Because parents are informal educators and teachers are the formal educators, the action taken by each is not necessarily the same; however, the action is directed toward the shared goal of supporting the student's learning and academic progress. Sharing of information and resources is often necessary to design and implement these interventions.

Shared Standards and Expectations

The level of expected performance held by key adults for the student is congruent across home and school, and reflects a belief that the student can learn and make academic progress.

▶ *Share Expectations and Suggestions-* The parent and teacher share expectations for the student's school performance (work completion, behavior, and achievement) and ask each other for suggestions on how to reinforce their message about expectations. These are communicated to the student.

▶ *Learning Goals Discussed-* The teacher, parent, and student articulate what they want the student to learn this year. Ambitious, but realistic, goals for the student are set through the use of parent, teacher, and student input. Consensus for learning goals in different subject areas is reached.

▶ *Create System for Displaying Expectations-* A system for concretely displaying the expectations for student performance as well as the student's progress toward meeting the learning goals is created so parents and educators reinforce the same message.

▶ *Reattribution Training-* Parents and educators use reattribution training by voicing their belief that the child can meet the standards and expectations if they try again, practice, and put forth effort.

▶ *Expectations Encouraged by Parents and*

Teachers- Teacher expectations are based on the level of student performance and are measurable and attainable. The parent supports the student and encourages him/her to strive for good grades (e.g., explain one thing learned in school today to the parent). The student is recognized for making academic progress.

Consistent Structure

The overall routine and monitoring provided by key adults for the student have been discussed and are congruent across home and school.

- *Create System for Monitoring Student Goals-* A system for both the parent and teacher to monitor the student's homework completion and/or academic progress toward the intended goal is developed.
- *Routines Shared-* Routines (i.e., schedule of daily events) at school and home are shared; ideally a "match" in style is achieved. If differences exist, they are discussed and clearly explained to the student.
- *Discipline Strategies Discussed-* With the goal of arriving at consensus about handling consequences of misbehavior or poor school performance, the parents and school personnel discuss discipline strategies.
- *Note System Created-* A home-school note system is used to maintain communication between home and school.
- *Contract Agreement-* A contract or partnership agreement is developed to ensure completion of homework.
- *Rules for Home and School are Reinforced-* Home and school rules are discussed, re-taught if necessary, and reinforced consistently.
- *Behavior is Agreed Upon-* The student clearly understands what behavior is and is not acceptable, and both the parent and teacher feel comfortable reminding the student of what he/she is to be doing (e.g., remember what we agreed upon).

Cross-setting Opportunity to Learn

The variety of learning options available to the student during school hours and outside time (i.e.,

home and community) supports the student's learning.

- *Provide a Rationale for Increasing Learning Opportunities Outside of School Hours-* For example, discuss how students spend 91% of their time from birth to age 18 outside of school, or students, once they begin kindergarten, spend 70% of their waking hours outside of school. Add to these statistics that high achievers spend more time outside of school engaged in constructive learning activities.
- *Determine Additional Learning Opportunities for the Student and Family-* Consider community, church, club, or internet activities that can be used to provide learning experiences.
- *The Student Lives in a Verbally-oriented World Both at Home and at School-* At home, the parents strive to enhance the amount of verbal interaction, and at school the student is given sufficient opportunity to respond.
- *Necessary Time Needed is Given-* The student is provided with the time needed to learn a skill or concept, and at home additional time for reinforcing the necessary skill or concept is provided.
- *Reading Materials are Varied-* Be sure that a variety of reading materials are present at home and at school.
- *Sufficient Practice is Provided-* Tasks at school provide the student with sufficient practice as well as opportunities for drill, practice, generalization, and transfer of information. Parents are aware of the amount and kind of practice needed for the student and reinforce what is taught at school.
- *Both the Teacher and the Parent Understand the Benefits of Mistakes-* Both the teacher and the parents require the student to correct his/her mistakes as part of the learning process.

Mutual Support

The guidance provided by, the communication between, and the interest shown by adults to facilitate the student's progress in school is effective.

Adults do these things on an ongoing basis to help the student learn and achieve.

▸ *Set Personal Goals-* The parent and teacher set personal goals with the student, and provide the student with regular, specific feedback regarding progress.

▸ *The Parent and Teacher Encourage the Student to Pursue Personal Interests and Academic Pursuits-* Teachers and parents should look for every possible opportunity to stress to students the importance of academic matters and being successful in their academic work.

▸ *Charting System Developed-* A charting/graphing system with respect to the student's academic progress is developed and shared across home and school.

▸ *The Parent and Teacher Call Each Other-* At the first sign of a concern or problem with respect to the student's learning and academic performance the parent and teacher will call each other.

▸ *The Parent and Teacher are Optimistic About the Student's Ability-* Parent and teacher express a belief that the student "can do it" if he/she uses his/her strengths and obtains the necessary support.

▸ *Share Observations-* The parent and teacher share their observations of the student's strengths and weaknesses in their respective contexts.

▸ *Develop an Action Plan-* The parent and teacher develop an action plan to provide the student with a consistent message about expectations for schoolwork, attendance, discipline, obtaining assistance with schoolwork, reinforcing home and school policies and practices, etc.

▸ *Develop Ways to Recognize and Praise the Student-* The parent and teacher develop realistic ways (e.g., tangible and social rewards; self-monitoring approaches) to recognize and praise the student.

▸ *Homework Center-* Organize an after-school homework center staffed by teachers and parents. Allow students to attend on an as needed basis.

▸ *Give Each Other Positive Feedback-* Provide frequent positive feedback to each other (parent to teacher, teacher to parent) when the student is behaving appropriately or showing improved academic progress.

▸ *Share Wishes and Worries-* Develop a "on the same page" philosophy by sharing wishes and worries about the student. Design a support system to address these issues.

Positive, Trusting Relationships

The amount of warmth and friendliness, praise and recognition, and the degree to which the adult-student relationship is positive and respectful is considered. How adults in the home, in the school, and in the community help the student to be a learner is also considered.

▸ *Get to Know Each Other-* The parent and teacher get to know each other before making educational decisions for the student.

▸ *Ample Time for Parent-teacher Communication is Provided-* The parent and teacher co-construct the "bigger picture" about the student's academic performance (e.g., behavior at home and school). Observations about the student are shared.

▸ *Discuss the Student's Strengths and Weaknesses-* Ensure that the parent and teacher are responsive to the student's needs and strive to develop a positive relationship with the student and between the teacher and parent. Ongoing communication focuses on how the system is working to enhance the student's academic progress.

▸ *Use Problem-Solving Techniques-* The parent and teacher agree to use problem solving as a structure for clarifying miscommunication. They call to check out a concern rather than become upset or blame the other party.

▸ *Positive Techniques are Used at Home and at School-* Effective communication, negotiation, anger management, and conflict resolution are used at home and at school to achieve family harmony and a cooperative classroom.

▸ *Use Problem-Solving Conferences-* Resolve home-school communication difficulties and address the needs of teachers and parents with respect to the student's schoolwork with problem-solving conferences.

► *Listen to the Student-* Both the parent and teacher listen to the student to understand his/her opinions, perspective, and needs.

► *Demonstrate Care for the Student-* The parent and teacher demonstrate genuine caring for the student and communicate to the student that they believe he/she is capable of improving in school (e.g., affirmations such as: "I believe . . .," "I have seen you . . .," etc.). Both refuse to give up on the student.

► *Demonstrate Problem-Solving Skills-* The parent and teacher demonstrate problem solving and negotiation skills for the student (e.g., use "think aloud" so the student understands the conclusion).

► *Admit When Wrong-* The parent and teacher admit when they are wrong and listen to suggestions from the student.

► *The Parent and Teacher Discuss Lessons Learned in Life and how Education has Assisted Them-* They take advantage of opportunities to describe their own lives and learning experiences and to talk to the student about the value of education.

Modeling

Parents and teachers demonstrate desired behaviors and commitment and value toward learning and working hard in their daily lives to the student.

► *Parents and Teachers Model the Value of Education-* Parents model the importance and value of education by using reading and math at home; similarly, the teacher is enthusiastic about the content that is being taught and models a "love for learning."

► *Discuss Value of Persistence-* The parent and teacher discuss with each other and the student what and/or how they are still learning, and that even when adults learn a new task, persistence is needed.

► *Set Personal Long-term Goals-* The parent and teacher set a personal long-term goal and use their progress toward the goal as an example of persistence and hard work.

► *Discuss Personal Values With Student-* Parents discuss with the student their values and the values they would like the student to have; the teacher reinforces the stated values.

CONCLUDING COMMENTS ABOUT INTERVENTION IMPLEMENTATION

There are several considerations that enhance the effectiveness of interventions that professionals put into place. The interventions should be as natural as possible. They should be put into place without lots of hubbub and distraction. Second, they should include empirically effective approaches. In this manual we have illustrated a number of interventions that have been researched and shown to be effective. Finally, the interventions that are put in place should be acceptable to those who implement them, and then put into place with good fidelity. Lentz, Allen, and Ehrhardt (1996) list a set of very important considerations for selection and implementation of interventions.

► Select interventions that are clearly related to the presenting problem (the referral concern) and that will lead to outcomes that alleviate the problem.

► Insure that the intervention goals directly overlap with the personal reasons for referral by the problem presenter.

► Design unobtrusive interventions; ones that "fit" the ecology.

► Design interventions so that those who referred the student will see progress or change toward alleviation of the referral concern.

► Work to have classroom environments support the changes you want to bring about in student behavior, and avoid short-term fixes.

► Use interventions for which there is good evidence of their effectiveness.

► Be ready to provide continual assistance; some students need it.

► Incorporate progress monitoring so you know whether movement toward goal accomplishment is evident.

► Keep a record of the interventions that work and of the conditions under which they work. You often will revisit such a record of effective interventions.

FUNCTIONAL
ASSESSMENT OF
ACADEMIC
BEHAVIOR

Reproducible Forms

Instructional Environment Checklist

Student	
Grade	Age
Content Area	
Examiner	

DIRECTIONS:

Based on information obtained using the data collection sources you selected (observation, recollection, record review, performance event), check the following areas for school and home intervention to address the specific referral concern. Summarize the top three things that need to be changed for the student to demonstrate greater academic success.

The *Instructional Environment Checklist* consists of three subscales: Instructional Support for Learning, Home Support for Learning, and Home-School Support for Learning. A complete picture of the student's needs comes from capturing both in-school and out-of-school factors that influence the student's performance in school. Furthermore, in considering the performance or progress the student has made or can make, it is critical to account for the degree of continuity in the home-school relationship.

INSTRUCTIONAL SUPPORT FOR LEARNING

☐ Instructional Match: The student's needs are assessed accurately and instruction is matched appropriately to the results of the instructional diagnosis.

☐ Instructional Expectations: There are realistic, yet high expectations for both the amount and accuracy of work to be completed by the student, and these are communicated clearly to the student.

☐ Classroom Environment: The classroom management techniques used are effective for the student; there is a positive, supportive classroom atmosphere; and, time is used productively.

☐ Instructional Presentation: Instruction is presented in a clear and effective manner; the directions contain sufficient information for the student to understand the kinds of behaviors or skills that are to be demonstrated; and, the student's understanding is checked.

☐ Cognitive Emphasis: Thinking skills and learning strategies for completing assignments are communicated explicitly to the student.

☐ Motivational Strategies: Effective strategies for heightening student interest and effort are used.

Student

❑ Relevant Practice: The student is given adequate opportunity to practice with appropriate materials and achieve a high success rate. Classroom tasks are clearly important to achieving instructional goals.

❑ Informed Feedback: The student receives relatively immediate and specific information on his/her performance or behavior; when the student makes mistakes, correction is provided.

❑ Academic Engaged Time: The student is actively engaged in responding to academic content; the teacher monitors the extent to which the student is actively engaged and redirects the student when the student is unengaged.

❑ Adaptive Instruction: The curriculum is modified within reason to accommodate the student's unique and specific instructional needs.

❑ Progress Evaluation: There is direct, frequent measurement of the student's progress toward completion of instructional objectives; data on the student's performance and progress are used to plan future instruction.

❑ Student Understanding: The student demonstrates an accurate understanding of what is to be done and how it is to be done in the classroom.

HOME SUPPORT FOR LEARNING

❑ Home Expectations and Attributions: High, realistic expectations about schoolwork are communicated to the child, and the value of effort and working hard in school is emphasized.

❑ Discipline Orientation: There is an authoritative (not permissive or authoritarian) approach to discipline, and the child is monitored and supervised by the parents.

❑ Home-affective Environment: The parent-child relationship is characterized by a healthy connectedness; it is generally positive and supportive.

❑ Parent Participation: There is an educative home environment, and others participate in the child's school and learning, at home and/or at school.

❑ Structure for Learning: Organization and daily routines facilitate the completion of schoolwork and support for the child's academic learning.

FUNCTIONAL
ASSESSMENT OF
ACADEMIC
BEHAVIOR

Student

HOME-SCHOOL SUPPORT FOR LEARNING

❑ Shared Standards and Expectations: The level of expected performance held by key adults for the student is congruent across home and school, and reflects a belief that the student can learn and make academic progress.

❑ Consistent Structure: The overall routine and monitoring provided by key adults for the student have been discussed and are congruent across home and school.

❑ Cross-setting Opportunity to Learn: The variety of learning options available to the student during school hours and outside time (i.e., home and community) supports the student's learning.

❑ Mutual Support: The guidance provided by, the communication between, and the interest shown by adults to facilitate the student's progress in school is effective. Adults do these things on an ongoing basis to help the student learn and achieve.

❑ Positive, Trusting Relationships: The amount of warmth and friendliness, praise and recognition, and the degree to which the adult-student relationship is positive and respectful is considered. How adults in the home, in the school, and in the community help the student to be a learner is also considered.

❑ Modeling: Parents and teachers demonstrate desired behaviors and commitment and value toward learning and working hard in their daily lives to the student.

FUNCTIONAL
ASSESSMENT OF
ACADEMIC
BEHAVIOR

Instructional Environment Checklist: Annotated Version

Student	
Grade	Age
Content Area	
Examiner	

The *Instructional Environment Checklist* consists of three subscales: Instructional Support for Learning, Home Support for Learning, and Home-School Support for Learning. A complete picture of the student's needs comes from capturing both in-school and out-of-school factors that influence the student's performance in school. Furthermore, in considering the student's performance or progress the student has made or can make, it is critical to account for the degree of continuity in the home-school relationship.

INSTRUCTIONAL SUPPORT FOR LEARNING

Instructional Match: The student's needs are assessed accurately and instruction is matched appropriately to the results of the instructional diagnosis.

- ❏ The student's level of skill development (e.g., entry-level skills) is assessed accurately.
- ❏ Instructional goals and objectives are matched to the student's skills.
- ❏ Assigned tasks are relevant in light of the student's background and experience.
- ❏ The student has the prerequisite skills necessary to complete assigned tasks.
- ❏ Timing and pacing of instruction is consistent with the student's skill level and attention span.
- ❏ Standards for acceptable daily classroom performance are consistent with the student's level of skill development.
- ❏ Skills necessary for the student to complete assigned tasks have been identified through task analysis.
- ❏ The student's success rate on academically relevant tasks is appropriate (i.e., 90-100% for independent work).

Student

Instructional Expectations: There are realistic, yet high expectations for both the amount and accuracy of work to be completed by the student, and these are communicated clearly to the student.

- ❏ The student understands what is expected of him/her (e.g., task completion, neatness, accuracy, and mastery of instructional goal).
- ❏ The student is expected to be an active and involved learner.
- ❏ The student is held accountable for his/her performance and progress.
- ❏ The student has sufficient opportunity for active responding.
- ❏ Objectives or goals for the instructional lesson are communicated clearly so that the student knows what is to be learned.

Classroom Environment: The classroom management techniques used are effective for the student; there is a positive, supportive classroom atmosphere; and, time is used productively.

- ❏ Classroom rules and routines are clearly understood by the student.
- ❏ The way in which rules are enforced enhances the likelihood that the student will comply with these rules.
- ❏ The student's compliance with the rules is continuously monitored.
- ❏ The student is able to manage his/her behavior.
- ❏ The student participates in establishment of classroom rules.
- ❏ Sufficient time is allocated to instruction such that it meets the student's needs.
- ❏ The student uses time productively (e.g., knows how to get help, procedures for breaks, where materials are).
- ❏ The classroom is a positive, safe, and cooperative environment for the student (e.g., there is a sense of belonging, connectedness, support, and acceptance by both teachers and peers).
- ❏ The student receives reminders about expected behavior in advance of a lesson.
- ❏ Classroom management allows for an academic focus (e.g., direct teaching of skills and concepts) and high rates of productivity (e.g., content coverage, work completion).

Instructional Presentation: Instruction is presented in a clear and effective manner; the directions contain sufficient information for the student to understand the kinds of behaviors or skills that are to be demonstrated; and, the student's understanding is checked.

- ❏ There is substantive teacher-student interaction (e.g., ask/answer questions, repeat directions, provide feedback).
- ❏ Directions are clear and of reasonable length/complexity for the student.
- ❏ The student's attention is focused and maintained on the critical skills and concepts to be learned.

FUNCTIONAL
ASSESSMENT OF
ACADEMIC
BEHAVIOR

Student

❑ Modeling and teacher demonstrations are sufficient for the student to be initially successful on independent activities.

❑ Both the teacher and student are enthusiastic about what is being taught.

❑ The instructional routine or presentation is varied.

❑ Information is structured for the student in a systematic way (e.g., advance organizers, review, guided practice).

Cognitive Emphasis: Thinking skills and learning strategies for completing assignments are communicated explicitly to the student.

❑ The student understands the purpose of the lesson.

❑ The learning strategies that are used (e.g., memorizing, reasoning, concluding, and evaluating) are effective for the student.

❑ The student can explain the process used to solve problems or complete work.

❑ The student knows why and how his/her responses are correct/incorrect.

Motivational Strategies: Effective strategies for heightening student interest and effort are used with the student.

❑ The student is encouraged to perform (e.g., shown how, told he/she can do the work).

❑ The value of learning is emphasized in addition to task completion.

❑ The student believes he/she can complete assigned tasks with success.

❑ The student understands the importance of tasks for future activities.

❑ Effective strategies to enhance student motivation have been considered:

    ❑ Relevance to background and personal experience

    ❑ The level of the task (not too high, not too low)

    ❑ Teacher interest and enthusiasm

    ❑ Ambitious but realistic goals

    ❑ Alternative ways to demonstrate mastery

    ❑ Rewards are contingent on mastery or a performance level at which the student can achieve with effort

    ❑ Reinforcement of student progress **and** achievement

FUNCTIONAL
ASSESSMENT OF
ACADEMIC
BEHAVIOR

Student

Relevant Practice: The student is given adequate opportunity to practice with appropriate materials and achieve a high success rate. Classroom tasks are clearly important in achieving instructional goals.

❑ The student is able to complete homework independently with 90% success.

❑ Practice activities assigned are directly connected to the student's instructional goal and are not just "busy work."

❑ Varied materials and different applications of skills taught are used to assist with generalization.

❑ The student has the opportunity to engage in enough drill work and repeated practice to make basic skills automatic.

❑ The kind of practice (guided, cooperative groups, independent) is appropriate for the student.

❑ There is sufficient student to student interaction.

❑ During seated activities, the student is engaged in varied and relevant work.

Informed Feedback: The student receives relatively immediate and specific information on his/her performance or behavior; when the student makes mistakes, correction is provided.

❑ After the correction of errors, the student has an immediate chance to practice a procedure or execute a task correctly.

❑ The student is lead to the correct answer through the use of error-correction procedures (i.e., cues and prompts) rather than being told the answer.

❑ When the student is confused or makes mistakes, the teacher uses a variety of alternative teaching methods to reexplain the task assigned.

❑ The student's errors are used to reteach skills or reexplain procedures.

❑ The student knows which skills he/she has mastered and which skills need more work.

❑ Praise and encouragement are specific, timely, and frequent.

❑ The student views the strategies used to assist him/her in dealing with failure as positive.

Academic Engaged Time: The student is actively engaged in responding to academic content; the teacher monitors the extent to which the student is actively engaged and redirects the student when the student is unengaged.

❑ Seatwork tasks (e.g., tutoring, peers, aides, and computers) promote active academic student responding.

❑ The student begins, attends to, and completes assigned work.

❑ The student spends little time sitting and waiting.

❑ The student promptly returns to work after breaks.

FUNCTIONAL
ASSESSMENT OF
ACADEMIC
BEHAVIOR

Student

❑ If the student is unengaged, student understanding of and interest in the assigned task is checked. And, there is a mechanism for the student to get help if needed.

❑ There are alternative options for the student when he/she is chronically unengaged.

❑ There are alternative tasks which can be assigned if the student finishes his/her work early.

❑ Questions or probes are directed to the student and the student gets frequent opportunities to respond.

Adaptive Instruction: The curriculum is modified within reason to accommodate the student's unique and specific instructional needs.

❑ Instruction is systematically adapted so that the student is able to experience success.

❑ Different materials, alternative teaching strategies, increased practice opportunities, or alternative group placements are considered when a student fails to master an objective.

❑ The effectiveness of alternative teaching strategies is monitored.

❑ The student receives additional review and practice in areas of difficulty.

❑ The student's needs, not only curriculum, are used to plan and modify instruction.

Progress Evaluation: There is direct, frequent measurement of the student's progress toward completion of instructional objectives; data on the student's performance and progress are used to plan future instruction.

❑ The student's success rate on assigned activities is frequently monitored. The student's engagement and attention are monitored as indicators of his/her understanding.

❑ Opportunities exist for the student to self-evaluate and self-monitor his/her work.

❑ Student progress and adaptations are monitored regularly and used to make adjustments in teaching strategies that better meet the needs of the student.

❑ The student-teacher ratio does not interfere with frequent monitoring of the student's performance.

❑ The student's progress through the curriculum is determined by degree of mastery of instructional objectives, rather than age, time in grade, or content covered.

Student Understanding: The student demonstrates an accurate understanding of what is to be done and how it is to be done in the classroom.

❑ The student understands instructional goals and mastery criteria.

❑ The student knows specific strategies to use to complete assigned work.

❑ The student demonstrates understanding of assigned tasks before, or shortly after beginning independent practice opportunities.

❑ The student is aware of his or her difficulties (e.g., lack of understanding or confusion) with assigned tasks.

FUNCTIONAL
ASSESSMENT OF
ACADEMIC
BEHAVIOR

Student

HOME SUPPORT FOR LEARNING

Home Expectations and Attributions: High, realistic expectations about schoolwork are communicated to the child, and the value of effort and working hard in school is emphasized.

❑ Expectations for performance (e.g., attendance, participation, and quality of performance) are realistic and clear to the child.

❑ The child is encouraged to put forth effort (e.g., "You can do it," "Practice is important," "Studying is important," "Keep trying.").

❑ The child knows that learning and school performance are important to his/her parents or caregivers.

❑ The child is told that he/she can do a good job in school.

❑ The child is told why school and learning are important.

Discipline Orientation: There is an authoritative (not permissive or authoritarian) approach to discipline, and the child is monitored and supervised by the parents.

❑ Clear, consistent rules and limits for the child's behavior are set.

❑ Negotiation/joint decision making occurs between the parent and the child.

❑ The child understands the rules, and the parent(s) follow through on delivery of consequences for rule compliance/infraction.

Home-affective Environment: The parent-child relationship is characterized by a healthy connectedness; it is generally positive and supportive.

❑ There is a warm, nurturing relationship between the parent(s) and the child.

❑ The parent(s) and child spend time together.

❑ The child is recognized for his/her performance and improvement.

❑ It is easy for the parent to find ways to recognize the child's accomplishments.

❑ If the child's grades are poor, parents do not express negative emotion, ignore the situation, or punish the child. Rather, they encourage the child.

❑ The child is encouraged to take new risks (try new things) in learning.

Parent Participation: There is an educative home environment, and others participate in the child's schooling and learning, at home and/or at school.

❑ The parents attend school functions.

❑ The parents communicate with school personnel.

❑ The parents are informed about their child's progress.

❑ The parents provide sufficient opportunity for the child to learn (the child is given opportunities to learn and to use school skills appropriately).

FUNCTIONAL
ASSESSMENT OF
ACADEMIC
BEHAVIOR

Student

❑ There is a literacy-rich environment (e.g., discussion of books, reading of books, discussion of TV programs or daily events; language errors are corrected; the child writes at home).

❑ Schoolwork is discussed at home (e.g., the child is asked about school every day).

Structure for Learning: Organization and daily routines facilitate the completion of schoolwork and support for the child's academic learning.

❑ There is constructive use of time (e.g., participation in positive learning activities like those that occur in sports, clubs, etc.).

❑ The child's schoolwork and use of out-of-school time are supervised and monitored.

❑ Regular routines exist, and time and a place to complete schoolwork/studying are available.

❑ Daily activities are organized/structured (e.g., the child knows the routine).

❑ Assistance with schoolwork (personal and materials) is available if needed.

❑ The child's out-of-school time is productive and does not interfere with learning activities.

❑ The parents or caregivers monitor the child's academic and behavioral performance and progress.

HOME-SCHOOL SUPPORT FOR LEARNING

Shared Standards and Expectations: The level of expected performance held by key adults for the student is congruent across home and school, and reflects a belief that the student can learn and make greater academic progress.

❑ Parents and educators have discussed and reached a consensus about expectations for student performance and standards for desired behavior.

❑ Parents and educators have set common goals for the student's performance.

❑ Parents and teachers have discussed expectations with the student.

❑ Parents and teachers emphasize the importance of student effort and persistence in the face of a challenge.

❑ Parents and teachers ensure the student understands the consequences for not meeting expectations.

Consistent Structure: The overall routine and monitoring provided by key adults for the student have been discussed and are congruent across home and school.

❑ A consistent routine is provided in the home (e.g., priority for schoolwork) and classroom (e.g., academic, task-oriented focus).

❑ Parents and teachers monitor student progress and supervise student's use of time.

❑ The student recognizes the consistency across home (e.g., authoritative parenting style) and school (e.g., classroom management) in terms of rules and interactions with the student.

FUNCTIONAL
ASSESSMENT OF
ACADEMIC
BEHAVIOR

Student

Cross-setting Opportunity to Learn: The variety of learning options available to the student during school hours and outside of school time (i.e., home and community) supports the student's learning.

❑ Learning occurs for the student at school and in the home.

❑ Home and school have communicated about ways to enhance student learning time (e.g., constructive learning activities).

Mutual Support: The guidance provided by, the communication between, and the interest shown by adults to facilitate the student's progress in school is effective. Adults do these things on an ongoing basis to help the student learn and achieve.

❑ Parents and educators encourage the student's academic interests and pursuits.

❑ Parents and educators show interest in what the student is learning and how he/she is performing.

❑ Home and school are available to assist the student's learning and each other in ways that help the student make progress.

Positive, Trusting Relationships: The amount of warmth and friendliness, praise and recognition, and the degree to which the adult-student relationship is positive and respectful is considered. How adults in the home, in the school, and in the community help the student to be a learner is also considered.

❑ The parent-student and teacher-student relationship is responsive to the student's needs and development.

❑ The student recognizes that both his/her parents and teachers care about him/her personally as well as his/her performance in school.

❑ Problem solving and nonblaming interactions exist between home and school, particularly when the student is experiencing academic or behavioral difficulties.

❑ Home and school trust each other; each is confident that the other partner is working to assist the student's learning.

Modeling: Parents and teachers demonstrate desired behaviors and commitment and value toward learning and working hard in their daily lives to the student.

❑ Parents and teachers discuss the importance and value of an education with the student.

❑ Parents and teachers model a commitment to learning and working hard in their daily lives.

FUNCTIONAL
ASSESSMENT OF
ACADEMIC
BEHAVIOR

Student

SUMMARY PROFILE FOR THE STUDENT

Ideas for Supporting the Student's Learning:

Two top ideas for instructional supports for learning are:

1. _____
2. _____

Two top ideas for home support for learning are:

1. _____
2. _____

Two top ideas for home-school support for learning are:

1. _____
2. _____

Summary of the Student's Support for Learning or Instructional Needs:

Across school and home contexts, the top 2-3 things that need to be changed for the student to demonstrate greater academic success are:

1. _____
2. _____
3. _____

FUNCTIONAL
ASSESSMENT OF
ACADEMIC
BEHAVIOR

Instructional Needs Checklist

Student _____

Grade _____   Age _____

Content Area _____

Examiner _____

INTRODUCTION

Teachers have the most comprehensive knowledge about how students respond to instruction and classroom expectations and demands. Important information for planning an instructional intervention or program includes understanding your experiences with this student. Information about the perception of the student's strengths and weaknesses, instructional needs, typical response to instruction, and instructional materials will be helpful in planning an intervention. To respond to these four areas, think about your experience teaching this student during the last month.

STEP 1: REFERRAL CONCERN

1. The three areas of greatest concern to me are:

_____

_____

_____

_____

_____

2. Areas that are instructional strengths for the student:

_____

_____

_____

_____

_____

STEP 2: INSTRUCTIONAL NEEDS

You have had the opportunity to observe the student under different instructional conditions. Think about his/her instructional needs. Check any areas in which you believe a change may be needed to provide the student with an optimal learning environment.

Planning Instruction for the Student

❑ Assigning tasks matched to student skill level

❑ Modifying classroom expectations to meet the student's needs

❑ Providing an appropriate student-teacher ratio

❑ Ensuring that the student understands the goals and strategies to complete assigned work

❑ Selecting appropriate curriculum materials

❑ Setting appropriate learning objectives for the student

Student

❑ Communicating learning goals to the student

❑ Making classroom assignments relevant for the student

❑ Ensuring opportunities for the student to be successful

❑ Getting the student actively engaged in learning

❑ Accounting for rate of progress and level of performance

Managing Instruction for the Student

❑ Amount of available instructional time

❑ Amount of time allocated to instruction

❑ Increasing opportunity to learn

❑ Making the classroom environment positive for the student

❑ Compliance with instructional routines

❑ Understanding of/compliance with classroom rules/consequences

❑ Decreasing inappropriate behavior

❑ Handling peer interactions

❑ Providing more structure

❑ Amount of homework

Delivering Instruction to the Student

❑ Strategies used to present lesson content

❑ Making task directions clear to and understood by the student

❑ Getting the student to understand lesson content

❑ Teaching specific learning strategies

❑ Strategies for focusing and maintaining student attention

❑ Amount of guided practice prior to independent practice

❑ Amount of relevant practice

❑ Appropriateness of independent seatwork activities

❑ Amount of teacher-student interaction available

❑ Examining ways to enhance motivation

❑ Getting the student to understand the importance (relevance) of tasks

❑ Giving informed feedback and opportunity to correct errors

❑ Helping the student persist on challenging tests

Monitoring and Evaluating Instruction for the Student

❑ Keeping students engaged in learning activities

FUNCTIONAL
ASSESSMENT OF
ACADEMIC
BEHAVIOR

Student

❑ Identifying strategies to get the student re-engaged when off task

❑ Measurement of the student's progress toward goals

❑ Adapting instruction to increase the student's success

❑ Amount of time needed to acquire new skills

❑ Amount of time needed to practice for mastery

Working With Families

❑ Setting appropriate expectations and learning goals across home and school

❑ Increasing the variety of learning opportunities across home and school

❑ Building a positive relationship between home and school

❑ Creating a common understanding about child behavior and discipline

❑ Engaging families at school and in the child's learning

❑ Identifying ways of mutual support between home and school

STEP 3: STUDENT RESPONSE TO TASKS

Teachers want students to spend time engaged in tasks they can perform with high success and that are directly relevant to learning goals. In your experience what has worked with this student?

❑ A clearly stated and specific lesson goal

❑ Explaining why the lesson is important to the student

❑ Using carefully sequenced instructional materials

❑ Sufficient time allocated to instruction

❑ Clear and frequently repeated directions for seatwork

❑ Step-by-step lesson explanation and more guided practice

❑ Emphasizing the importance of student effort and practice for success

❑ Ensuring that the student can do the work (appropriate skill match)

❑ Ensuring that the student is interested in the work

❑ Asking the student many questions about his/her work

❑ Using prompts and cues to assist or expand the student's response

❑ Asking the student to explain his/her answer or process used

❑ Checking independent seatwork immediately and frequently

❑ Varying the practice activities

❑ Telling the student why his/her answer is correct/incorrect

❑ Informing the student of his/her progress toward the learning goal

❑ Including the student in the choice of tasks

FUNCTIONAL
ASSESSMENT OF
ACADEMIC
BEHAVIOR

Student

STEP 4: INSTRUCTIONAL TASKS AND MATERIALS

Assigned tasks and instructional materials are primary ways to reinforce teacher instruction.

1. On what kinds of tasks does the student perform best?

- ❑ Cooperative learning
- ❑ Peer-assisted learning
- ❑ Highly structured
- ❑ Independent seatwork
- ❑ Creative paper-pencil
- ❑ Reading
- ❑ Verbal discussion
- ❑ Worksheets requiring recall (e.g., fill in the blank)
- ❑ Worksheets requiring recognition (e.g., multiple choice, true/false)
- ❑ Tasks reinforcing one skill
- ❑ Tasks reinforcing multiple skills
- ❑ Simple cognitive demands (e.g., locating facts, matching)
- ❑ Complex cognitive demands (e.g., drawing conclusions)

2. On what kinds of materials does the student perform best?

- ❑ Workbooks
- ❑ Readers
- ❑ Manipulatives
- ❑ Computer-assisted instruction
- ❑ Interactive teaching programs
- ❑ Projects
- ❑ Self-discovery
- ❑ Discussion

STEP 5: INSTRUCTIONAL MODIFICATIONS

Check those instructional modifications that you consider to be most feasible in your classroom.

- ❑ Pace of instruction
- ❑ Grouping arrangements
- ❑ Selection of materials
- ❑ Kind of assigned tasks
- ❑ Instructional goals/objectives

FUNCTIONAL
ASSESSMENT OF
ACADEMIC
BEHAVIOR

Student

- ❑ Amount of practice and review
- ❑ Feedback/reinforcement systems
- ❑ Motivational systems
- ❑ Grading/progress evaluation
- ❑ Demonstration/modeling/examples provided
- ❑ Sequence of instruction
- ❑ Task directions
- ❑ Checking for student understanding
- ❑ Supplemental instruction

STEP 6: IF ONLY TWO THINGS COULD BE DONE FOR THIS STUDENT, WHAT WOULD THEY BE?

1. _____

2. _____

STEP 7. OTHER OBSERVATIONS/RELEVANT INFORMATION

FUNCTIONAL
ASSESSMENT OF
ACADEMIC
BEHAVIOR

Parental Experience With Their Child's Learning and Schoolwork

Child's Name

Grade

Parent(s) Name

INTRODUCTION:

Parents observe how their child responds to schoolwork and classroom expectations and demands. They also know about their child's schooling experiences across grades. They have also tried many ways to encourage their child to learn. It is important to understand their experiences and observations if a coordinated intervention or program between home and school is going to be planned.

STEP 1: REFERRAL CONCERN

1. Check any concerns you have for your child's academic performance:

❑ Reading difficulties

❑ Attitude about schoolwork and learning

❑ Following directions

❑ Completing homework

❑ Attending to his/her schoolwork

❑ Maintaining a study schedule

❑ Knowing what to do on an assignment

❑ Making friends

❑ Skill level

❑ Taking responsibility for schoolwork

❑ Organizational skills

❑ Completing tasks on time

❑ Amount of homework

❑ Level of assigned schoolwork

❑ Spends little time studying

❑ Needs extra assistance

❑ Spend too much time watching TV

❑ Sports/extracurricular activities interfere with schoolwork

❑ Others:_____

Student

2. My child has been most successful in school when:

_____

_____

_____

3. My child's strengths and interests are:

_____

_____

_____

STEP 2: YOUR OBSERVATIONS

What is true for your experiences with your child's academic performance?

▶ Teachers care about my child.	Yes	No
▶ School personnel do a good job of keeping me well informed of my child's progress.	Yes	No
▶ School personnel want my ideas when a concern surfaces about my child.	Yes	No
▶ I understand classroom rules and expectations.	Yes	No
▶ There are sufficient opportunities for my child's teachers and I to communicate about my child.	Yes	No

At home I've noticed:

▶ My child complains about school.	Yes	No
▶ My child knows I am concerned about his/her school experience.	Yes	No
▶ My child is encouraged to work hard in school, to put forth a lot of effort, and to try again.	Yes	No
▶ My child and I discuss the importance of attendance and participation in the classroom.	Yes	No
▶ My child knows that learning/education is a priority in our home.	Yes	No
▶ My child knows that school is important and that he/she is expected to work hard.	Yes	No
▶ My child and I talk about how he/she is doing/learning in school.	Yes	No
▶ My child and I talk about what is going on at school.	Yes	No

FUNCTIONAL
ASSESSMENT OF
ACADEMIC
BEHAVIOR

Student

- ▶ My child knows I know how he/she is doing in the classroom. — Yes — No

- ▶ My child usually needs help with schoolwork. — Yes — No

- ▶ My child knows I'll call school when I have a question or concern. — Yes — No

- ▶ My child and I talk about how to be a good student. — Yes — No

- ▶ My child and I talk about working hard when things are tough. — Yes — No

- ▶ My child's behavior/performance improves when I am involved. — Yes — No

- ▶ My child and I can talk about schoolwork and his/her overall school performance without intense anger. — Yes — No

- ▶ My child knows he/she is not performing in school as well as other children in the family. — Yes — No

- ▶ My child enjoys learning extra things at home from his/her parents or siblings. — Yes — No

- ▶ Explaining schoolwork to my child often results in crying or conflict. — Yes — No

*Thank you for sharing your observations about your child and
his/her schoolwork and school-related behavior!*

FUNCTIONAL
ASSESSMENT OF
ACADEMIC
BEHAVIOR

▶ *Intervention Documentation Record*

Name _____ Grade _____

Teacher _____

Case Coordinator _____

Date _____

Intervention Planning Team Members _____

Referral Concern: Describe in specific, observable behavior, what the student does and what educators want the student to do.

Current Academic Behavior	Desired Academic Behavior
_____	_____
_____	_____
_____	_____
_____	_____
_____	_____

Previous Interventions:

Date	Description	Effect
_____	_____	_____
_____	_____	_____
_____	_____	_____
_____	_____	_____
_____	_____	_____
_____	_____	_____

Summary of the Student's Support for Learning or Instructional Needs:
Across school and home contexts, the top 2-3 things that need to be changed for the student to demonstrate greater academic success are:

1. _____

2. _____

3. _____

	Student

Intervention Actions Taken:

What	By Whom	Where	Duration of Intervention
_____	_____	_____	_____
_____	_____	_____	_____
_____	_____	_____	_____
_____	_____	_____	_____
_____	_____	_____	_____
_____	_____	_____	_____
_____	_____	_____	_____

Evidence for Success:

_____

_____

_____

_____

_____

Other Recommendations:

_____

_____

_____

_____

_____

FUNCTIONAL
ASSESSMENT OF
ACADEMIC
BEHAVIOR

▶ *Observation Record*

Student	
Grade	Age
Content Area	
Date of Observation	
Length of Observation	
Examiner	

STEP 1

Before describing the student's response to instruction, find out what is being taught, what is the goal of the lesson, and where the lesson is placed in the instructional sequence.

What is the content of instruction?

_____

_____

_____

_____

What is the goal of the lesson?

_____

_____

_____

_____

Placement in lesson sequence:

❑ New, introductory   ❑ New, plus initial practice   ❑ Practice   ❑ Review

STEP 2

Remember: The target student is the focus of the observation. Using the 12 instructional environment components as a systematic way to observe, observe the student in relation to the task characteristics and instructional and management strategies used. Record relevant observations (e.g., student's response to instruction), ideas for intervention, and additional questions that may help the collaborative team design an intervention for the target student.

Student

INSTRUCTIONAL PLANNING

▶ Instructional Match

▶ Teacher Expectations

How are the student's performance and behavior affected by instructional planning?

_____

_____

_____

_____

_____

INSTRUCTIONAL MANAGEMENT

▶ Classroom Environment

How are the student's performance and behavior affected by instructional management?

_____

_____

_____

_____

_____

INSTRUCTIONAL DELIVERY

▶ Instructional Presentation

▶ Cognitive Emphasis

▶ Motivational Strategies

▶ Relevant Practice

▶ Informed Feedback

How is the student's performance and behavior affected by instructional delivery?

_____

_____

_____

_____

_____

INSTRUCTIONAL MONITORING AND EVALUATION

▶ Academic Engaged Time

▶ Adaptive Instruction

▶ Progress Evaluation

▶ Student Understanding

How are the student's performance and behavior affected by instructional monitoring and evaluation?

_____

_____

_____

_____

_____

FUNCTIONAL
ASSESSMENT OF
ACADEMIC
BEHAVIOR

▶ *Student Interview Record*

Student	
Grade	Age
Content Area	
Date	
Examiner	

INTRODUCTION:

Students like to talk about their schoolwork, and their perceptions are valuable in designing interventions. This semistructured interview format allows the examiner to gather information of both the student's perception of the assigned task during the classroom observation and the student's perception of assignments during the last month. Also, the semistructured interview format allows the examiner to pursue individualized questions with the student. Rewording of questions may be necessary, and if so, is encouraged

INSTRUCTIONS

I want to find out what you think about your schoolwork; things like how hard it is, how easy it is, what your teacher wants you to do, what helps you learn and get your work done. I have some questions, but I want you to tell me anything "extra" you would like.

STEP 1

Directions for Assigned Task During Classroom Observation: I have some questions for you about the work you were doing today in _____. (The examiner should have the work available.)

1. I want you to tell me what you needed to do on this assignment (or these assignments).

    a. What did your teacher want you to learn?_____

    b. What did your teacher tell you about why this assignment is important?

    _____

    c. What did you have to do? _____

    d. Show me how you did the work. (Have the student explain a sample item.)

    _____

2. I am going to ask you several questions. In each case, I want you to tell me your answer by answering "Yes," "No," or "Kind of."

	YES	NO	KIND OF
a. I understood this assignment.			
b. I believed I could do the assignment.			
c. This assignment was interesting.			
d. This assignment was different than most of my assignments.			

Student

3. Knowledge of strategies for assigned task:

    a. (Declarative Knowledge)—Do you know of any ways to go about this assignment to make it easier? _____

    b. (Procedural Knowledge)—How do you do that? _____

    c. (Conditional Knowledge)—When would you use that? Why would you bother to do that? _____

4. Student success rate (recorded by the examiner): _____

STEP 2

Directions for Assignments During the Last Month: I want you to think about your work in this class. Think about the kind of work you've had for the last month. Answer "Yes," "No," or "Sometimes" to my questions.

1. Context of Instruction

	YES	NO	SOME-TIMES
a. My assignments are interesting to me.			
b. I can get most of the answers correct on my assignments.			
c. I want to do a good job on assignments.			
d. I do a good job on assignments.			
e. I get enough time to do my work.			
f. My teacher calls on me to answer questions in class.			

2. Understanding of Assignments

	YES	NO	SOME-TIMES
a. I know how to complete my assignments.			
b. I usually need lots of help from my teacher to understand what I have to do.			

3. Student Accountability for Learning

	YES	NO	SOME-TIMES
a. I do my schoolwork when I'm supposed to.			
b. I try hard to complete my work, but I don't always get it done.			
c. I answer questions in class.			
d. I ask for help when I need it or when I have a question about the assignment.			

    e. I am successful at my schoolwork when:

      1. _____

      2. _____

      3. _____

FUNCTIONAL
ASSESSMENT OF
ACADEMIC
BEHAVIOR

Student _____

4. Teacher Expectations

	YES	NO	SOME-TIMES
a. I know what my teacher expects me to do.			
b. I know when I'm confused.			
c. I know what to do when I'm finished with my work.			

d. What happens when your work isn't done or you make lots of mistakes?

_____

_____

5. Student Cognitions (Answer "Yes," "No," "Sometimes," or "Don't know.")

a. When you're learning new skills or ideas:

	YES	NO	SOME-TIMES	DON'T KNOW
1. Do you listen closely to what the teacher says?				
2. Do you miss important things your teacher says because you aren't paying attention?				
3. Do you think about things you learned in the past that are like the new things the teacher is talking about?				

b. When your teacher talks about things you don't understand:

	YES	NO	SOME-TIMES	DON'T KNOW
1. Do you stop listening and start to think about other things?				
2. Do you just forget about it and listen to what the teacher says next?				
3. Can you figure out exactly what it is that you don't understand?				

c. When your teacher asks other students questions during class:

	YES	NO	SOME-TIMES	DON'T KNOW
Do you figure out the answers?				

d. When you are doing your schoolwork:

	YES	NO	SOME-TIMES	DON'T KNOW
1. Do you find out that you didn't understand the lesson as well as you thought you did while the teacher was teaching?				
2. Do you think about how the teacher worked similar problems or examples?				
3. Do you know if you have done your work right or wrong?				

FUNCTIONAL
ASSESSMENT OF
ACADEMIC
BEHAVIOR

Student

e. What do you do when you can't do your schoolwork?

_____

_____

f. Do you learn more if you do some extra work at home? ☐ Yes ☐ No

g. Is there anything else you want to tell me about your schoolwork?

_____

_____

FUNCTIONAL
ASSESSMENT OF
ACADEMIC
BEHAVIOR

▶ *Teacher Interview Record*

Student	
Grade	Age
Date	
School	
Teacher	
Examiner	

INSTRUCTIONS

It is important for me to understand what it is like to have _____ as a student in your classroom, what it is like to teach him/her every day. I have some questions about _____'s instruction that will help me to better understand your experience with him/her.

1. **Typical Performance**   How typical was _____'s performance on _____?

2. **Instructional Goal**   When I observed _____ in _____, you told me the goal of the lesson was _____.

   a. Do you have other instructional goals for _____?
   Explain: _____
   _____
   _____

   b. How do your goals differ from those for his/her classmates? _____
   _____
   _____
   _____

Student

3. Expectations

What have you told _____ about your expectations for:
a. Classroom participation?
b. Completing tasks?
c. Neatness?
d. Accuracy?
e. Obtaining assistance?
f. General behavior?
Do you call on _____ during class discussion? _____
What happens? _____
_____
_____

4. Planning Instruction

What information have you used to plan assignments for _____?
_____
What other information do you think we need to plan assignments?
_____
_____

5. Instructional Placement

a. What is _____'s success rate on assignments?

b. How would you describe _____'s task completion rate?
☐ Low   ☐ Moderate   ☐ High
c. How would you describe _____'s time on task?
☐ Low   ☐ Moderate   ☐ High
d. How did you decide where to place _____ in the curriculum?
_____
_____

e. Do you think there is a good match between _____'s
skill level and the demand on the assignments? _____
Tell me more. _____
_____

6. Independent Assignments

a. How much time does _____ have to practice?
b. Does _____ work alone or with others?
c. What kinds of assignments can _____ handle most successfully?
d. Do _____'s seatwork assignments vary from day to day or week to week? _____
Tell me more. _____
_____

7. Evaluate Progress

a. How do you check/monitor _____'s progress?
b. How does _____ compare to other students in achieving your goals?
c. Does _____ need more time to learn than the curriculum allows?
_____ How much more time is needed for _____ to learn than
for his/her peers? _____
_____

FUNCTIONAL
ASSESSMENT OF
ACADEMIC
BEHAVIOR

Student

8. Overall Success Rate

(Obtained From Teacher)   a. For new, introductory assigned tasks:

i. Relative to peers, estimate the student's percentage of assignments completed (regardless of accuracy).

❏ 0-49%   ❏ 50-70%   ❏ 71-99%   ❏ 100%

ii. Relative to peers, estimate the student's accuracy of completed assignments (i.e., % correct of work done).

❏ 0-49%   ❏ 50-70%   ❏71-99%   ❏ 100%

b. For independent practice tasks:

i. Relative to peers, estimate the student's percentage of assignments completed (regardless of accuracy).

❏ 0-49%   ❏ 50-70%   ❏ 71-99%   ❏ 100%

ii. Relative to peers, estimate the student's accuracy of completed assignments (i.e., % correct of work done).

❏ 0-49%   ❏ 50-70%   ❏ 71-99%   ❏ 100%

9. Is there anything else I should know about _____'s instruction?

_____
_____
_____
_____
_____
_____
_____

FUNCTIONAL
ASSESSMENT OF
ACADEMIC
BEHAVIOR

FUNCTIONAL ASSESSMENT OF ACADEMIC BEHAVIOR

▶ *Parent Interview Record*

Student	
Grade	Age
Date	
Parent Interviewed	
Examiner (if other than parent)	

INTRODUCTION:

As a parent, you make important observations about your child and his/her school-work and school-related behaviors. This information can help us create the best learning experience for your child. There are many questions included on this form. Remember, no parent does all of these things. And not all of these things may be important to help your child learn. Also, feel free to add any information you think we should know about your child.

STEP 1

General observations: Answer "**Yes**," "**No**," or "**Sometimes**" to these questions. Answer "**Yes**" if it happens about 80% of the time (4 out of 5 days). Answer "**No**" if it happens about 20% of the time (1 out of 5 days). Answer "**Sometimes**" if it is in the middle (happening about 2 or 3 days per week). Answer "**Don't Know**" if you cannot select one of the other choices.

1. My child understands his/her schoolwork in:

	YES	NO	SOME-TIMES	DON'T KNOW
a. Reading				
b. Math				
c. Social Studies				
d. Science				
e. Language				
f. Spelling				
g. Other: _____				

2. My child has difficulty:

	YES	NO	SOME-TIMES	DON'T KNOW
a. Memorizing				
b. Following directions				
c. Attending to his/her schoolwork				
d. Completing homework				
e. Maintaining a study schedule				
f. Completing assigned chores				
g. Understanding what is read				
h. Completing projects				
i. Knowing what to do on an assignment				

Student

3. At home I've noticed:

	YES	NO	SOME-TIMES	DON'T KNOW
a. My child and I talk about what is going on at school.				
b. My child and I can talk about how he/she is doing in school.				
c. My child complains about school.				
d. My child knows I'm concerned about his/her school performance.				
e. My child and I can talk about schoolwork and his/her overall school performance without intense anger.				
f. My child knows he/she is not performing in school as well as other children in the family.				
g. My child has the necessary materials to complete schoolwork at home.				
h. My child enjoys learning extra things at home from his/her parents or siblings.				
i. Explaining schoolwork to my child often results in crying or conflict.				
j. I offer to help with schoolwork.				
k. I tutor my child at home.				

STEP 2

Specific Observations: Check any statement that is fairly typical of your child or present in your home (i.e., happens often).

❑ Completing schoolwork is part of my child's daily routine.

❑ My child is encouraged to have an "I can do it" attitude.

❑ My child is encouraged to work hard in school, to put forth a lot of effort, and to try again.

❑ Someone at home helps organize my child's assignments.

❑ In our home, my child's efforts are praised.

❑ The importance of attendance and participation in the classroom is discussed with my child.

❑ My child is told he/she is expected to behave and perform at school.

❑ My child is told that school is important.

❑ My child knows that learning is a priority in our home.

❑ My child knows that school performance is improved through effort and practice.

❑ My child understands my expectations for his/her school performance.

❑ My child's out-of-school activities are monitored.

FUNCTIONAL
ASSESSMENT OF
ACADEMIC
BEHAVIOR

Student

❑ My child and I make joint decisions about my child's behavior and use of time.

❑ Rules are enforced in our home.

❑ My child's progress and improvement are recognized.

❑ My child is rewarded for good grades.

❑ My child's schoolwork is viewed on a weekly basis.

❑ Clear and consistent limits for my child's behavior (e.g., where he/she can go, how late he/she can be out, with whom he/she can go places) are set.

❑ How best to discipline my child is clear to me.

❑ If my child's grades are poor, I am not inclined to express negative emotion, ignore the situation, or punish my child.

❑ My child completes his/her chores or responsibilities at home.

❑ My child follows my requests/rules most of the time.

❑ My child understands the household rules and expectations.

❑ My child and I have a good and generally positive relationship (e.g., we get along pretty well).

❑ I talk about my child's strengths with my child.

❑ I try to understand my child's needs and point of view.

❑ My child and I spend some relaxing time together on a regular basis.

❑ My child is encouraged to try new things (i.e., take risks in learning).

❑ When my child has a problem, we discuss it.

❑ Opportunities are created for my child's interests.

❑ My child uses reading, math, and writing skills at home.

❑ My child and I talk about schoolwork in our home.

❑ I communicate with school personnel (e.g., notes, phone calls, conferences).

❑ I cooperate with the school on issues of schoolwork, discipline, and attendance.

❑ My child's language errors are corrected at home.

❑ I discuss books, stories, and TV programs with my child.

❑ My child is encouraged to read for fun.

❑ I participate in school activities and attend school functions.

❑ My child has opportunities to solve problems at home.

❑ I stay informed about my child's progress.

❑ In our home my child and I make learning fun (e.g., using math in cooking, reading to find an answer to a question).

❑ My child and I have conversations about daily events in our neighborhood or the world.

❑ My child and I read (e.g., adults read in the presence of the child, the child reads for pleasure, adults read to the child).

❑ My child has reading materials available (e.g., own books, uses the library).

❑ My child sees adults and siblings learning new things.

❑ Regular routines and schedules exist and daily activities are organized for my child.

FUNCTIONAL
ASSESSMENT OF
ACADEMIC
BEHAVIOR

Student

☐ Resources for studying/learning are available to my child at home.

☐ Someone is available to help my child learn at home.

☐ When my child is having trouble with homework, assistance is available.

☐ My child's homework is checked for accuracy and completion.

☐ I would provide rewards for homework completion if directed by school personnel.

☐ I limit the amount of my child's TV watching.

☐ My child has a place for studying.

☐ My child knows I am available to help with schoolwork.

☐ My child participates in other activities (sports, music, clubs) during out-of-school hours.

☐ A routine for homework completion (e.g., quiet study place, a schedule) has been established.

STEP 3

In closing:

1. List some things that you and your child enjoy doing together.

   _____

   _____

2. Parents have many demands in their lives. However, check if you could help assist your child's learning in school by:

   ☐ Rewarding or reinforcing your child's accomplishment

   ☐ Establishing a specific study time

   ☐ Increasing your conversations about schoolwork

   ☐ Teaching your child something new on a regular basis

   ☐ Spending more time with your child in enrichment activities (e.g., the library, park, museum)

   ☐ Reading together on a regular basis

   ☐ Reviewing math skills (e.g., math facts) on a regular basis

   ☐ Practicing spelling words on a regular basis

   ☐ Assisting your child in writing letters

   ☐ Talking more frequently with your child's teacher(s)

   ☐ Planning a specific instructional program to be carried out in home and school

   ☐ Supplementing school learning with short homework activities at home

   ☐ Helping your child complete his/her assignments

   ☐ Monitoring your child's academic progress

   ☐ Establishing a learning contract with your child and your child's teacher(s)

3. Is there anything else we should know about your child and his/her schoolwork?

   _____

   _____

   _____

FUNCTIONAL
ASSESSMENT OF
ACADEMIC
BEHAVIOR

► *Supplemental Teacher
Interview Questions*

Student	
Grade	Age
Content Area	
Examiner	

This section provides a list of additional questions for some of the FAAB components to be used when interviewing the teacher. The examiner is encouraged to supplement the Teacher Interview Record with these provided questions, to reword these questions, and to create other questions to help in rating the FAAB components.

COMPONENT 1. INSTRUCTIONAL MATCH

Instructional Diagnosis

1. Tell me how you determine _____'s instructional needs.
2. What did you need to know about _____ before beginning this lesson or unit?
3. How do you determine _____'s skill level?
4. When do you communicate these rules?
5. How do you handle classroom disruptions due to inappropriate behavior?
6. What are the necessary prerequisite skills needed to perform the task?
   a. Which of these has _____ mastered?
   b. Which of these might cause _____ trouble?
7. How is the average student in your class doing on the task?
8. How discrepant is _____ from the average performance?
9. How many different activities are there in the lesson?
10. What are the various cognitive/thinking demands of the task (e.g., discrimination recognition, recall, sequencing, categorizing, inferring, explaining, applying)?
11. What must the student know in order to be successful on the lesson, task, or unit?

Instructional Prescription

1. How do you determine the appropriate instructional level for _____?
2. How does your instructional planning differ for _____ than for your other students?
3. What methods are most effective to use with_____ to meet your objectives?
4. What materials are most effective to use with _____ to meet your objectives?
5. How is your instructional planning affected by the district's adopted curriculum objectives?
6. How is your instructional planning affected by the district's adopted textbooks/materials?
7. Tell me how you plan instruction for _____.
8. What skills do you want the student to learn?
9. What is your instructional goal for _____?
10. Do _____'s learning characteristics affect your choice of tasks or materials? If so, how?

_____

Student

11. What is the sequence of activities that you believe will be necessary for _____ to cover the skill?

12. Is there anything special or different you have to do when teaching _____?

13. What are _____'s characteristics that interfere with successful mastery of your objectives?

14. What are _____'s characteristics that assist him/her in meeting your objectives?

15. Are the scope and sequences of the material clearly specified?

16. Are facts/concepts/skills sequenced from simple to complex?

17. Why did you select this skill or goal for _____?

18. Was there anything about _____'s personality or the way _____ learns that affected your choice of materials, the kind of assignment, or the teaching method?

19. When you planned the lesson for _____, did you think any parts of the lesson would be difficult for him/her? If yes, what parts? How do you plan to handle these tough spots?

20. Do you have a specified scope and sequence? Do you have a planned list of instructional objectives (i.e., skills) to be taught?

21. What is your goal for _____? Is the goal the same for all your students? How does the goal vary for _____ from the other students? Why was this goal selected?

COMPONENT 2. INSTRUCTIONAL EXPECTATIONS

1. What are your expectations for _____?

    a. For task completion?

    b. For accuracy?

    c. For neatness?

2. How do you communicate your expectations to _____?

3. How do you determine what is a realistic expectation for _____?

4. What do you want _____ to do if he/she finishes early, is confused, and/or needs to ask for help? How do you communicate these to _____?

5. What are the usual things you do when _____ does not do a good job on his/her assignment?

6. What is the usual thing you do if _____ does not complete assigned work?

7. What is an acceptable standard of performance for _____?

8. How do you check to see that _____ reached this standard?

9. Did _____ know what you expected of him/her during this lesson? How do you know?

10. Do you have a set standard that you will require _____ to reach by the end of this unit?

11. Do you have the same expectations for _____ as you have for your other students? If not, what is different?

12. What expectations do you have for _____ regarding classroom participation?

13. What happens if any of your expectations are unfulfilled?

14. What do you do if _____'s work is of poorer quality than you expect?

15. What are the consequences if _____'s behavior is not acceptable?

FUNCTIONAL
ASSESSMENT OF
ACADEMIC
BEHAVIOR

Student

COMPONENT 3. CLASSROOM ENVIRONMENT

Classroom Management

1. What rules do you have for appropriate behavior in your classroom?
2. Why are these rules important?
3. How do you communicate these rules to your class?
4. When do you communicate these rules?
5. How do you handle classroom disruptions due to inappropriate behavior?

Productive Time Use

1. What routines do you have for nonacademic business—things like:
   a. Use of materials,
   b. Bathroom breaks,
   c. Use of free time, and
   d. Transitions between lessons?
2. How do you communicate these routines to your class?

COMPONENT 5. COGNITIVE EMPHASIS

1. What learning strategies have you taught _____ to use in completion of his/her tasks?
2. How much have you stressed thinking skills with _____?
3. What success have you had in teaching _____ how to think through the process or operations of a task?

COMPONENT 6. MOTIVATIONAL STRATEGIES

1. How do you motivate _____?
2. Which methods have been most effective?
3. When are additional motivational techniques necessary?
4. What kinds of motivational techniques have you tried?

COMPONENT 7. RELEVANT PRACTICE

Practice Opportunity

1. Are practice and review of content material provided? How frequently?
2. Are these appropriate practice opportunities that lead to mastery of skills/concepts?
3. Is there enough practice for a slow or disabled learner (if applicable)?
4. Can the student complete the assigned practice work independently?
5. Is regular feedback provided so that the probability of error is reduced in independent practice activities?
6. Do you ever give homework? If so, when? What do you give for homework?
7. How much of the student's day is spent in seatwork activities?
8. How much time is scheduled for practice?
9. What kinds of tasks do you use for _____ to practice?
10. Do you plan to include speed and accuracy drills?

© 2002 by Sopris West. All rights reserved. Published by Sopris West (800) 547-6747.
(*Functional Assessment of Academic Behavior: Creating Successful Learning Environments, 168 FAAB*).

FUNCTIONAL
ASSESSMENT OF
ACADEMIC
BEHAVIOR

Student

Task Relevance

1. How is the content of the lesson presentation consistent with your stated objectives?
2. How is the independent seatwork practice assignment consistent with the content of the lesson presentation?
3. How is the independent seatwork assignment important for the student's attainment of the stated goal?
4. Are any of the practice assignments "busy work" and/or used to control the student?
5. How does the assigned work review or reinforce the student's skill in the most efficient way?
6. How are practice opportunities directly related to desired outcomes?

Instructional Material

1. What is the student's success rate on the assigned instructional materials?
2. What materials are used for practice?
3. Are any supplemental materials available or used? If so, which materials?
4. What kinds of instructional materials have been used with _____? Which are most or least effective?

COMPONENT 9. ACADEMIC ENGAGED TIME

1. What do you expect the student to do if he/she needs help with seatwork?
2. If you notice that _____ is off task, how do you refocus his/her attention?

COMPONENT 10. ADAPTIVE INSTRUCTION

1. If _____ does not understand the assignment, despite several attempts to re-explain the task, what do you do?
2. What alternative teaching strategies or modifications do you routinely consider implementing for _____?
3. When _____ is experiencing ongoing difficulty in learning the intended material, what strategies do you employ to facilitate his/her performance?
4. What provisions have you made in the physical arrangement of the classroom to accommodate _____?
5. If _____ cannot stay with the pace of group instruction, how do you solve this problem?
6. Do you use any special teaching techniques for _____ to do well on this task?
7. What alternative teaching strategies are used for _____ when he/she fails to master an objective?
8. What kinds of modifications are feasible to meet _____'s individual needs?
9. Which of these modifications are feasible for _____ in your room:
   a. Change in materials?
   b. Change teaching methods?
   c. Change the task?
   d. Change the goal?
   e. Provide extra practice, reviews?
   f. Change feedback procedures?
10. Which modifications have been effective with _____?
11. How have you evaluated these methods to know which ones are successful with him/her?
12. Does _____ require any modifications to complete the task successfully?

FUNCTIONAL
ASSESSMENT OF
ACADEMIC
BEHAVIOR

(Functional Assessment of Academic Behavior: Creating Successful Learning Environments, 168 FAAB).

Student

COMPONENT 11. PROGRESS EVALUATION

Monitoring Student Progress

What kinds of records do you keep to monitor _____'s progress?

Follow-Up Planning

1. How do you decide whether _____ needs to be retaught the skill or is ready to move on to another skill?

2. Did _____ meet your objective? How did you determine this?

3. What do you plan to teach next? Why have you chosen this?

4. What factors do you take into account in deciding whether to move on to the next unit (curriculum objective or skill)?

FUNCTIONAL
ASSESSMENT OF
ACADEMIC
BEHAVIOR

▶ *Supplemental Student
Interview Questions*

Student	
Grade	Age
Content Area	
Examiner	

This section provides additional questions for some of the FAAB components that a team member may want to ask to understand the student's instructional experience. The examiner is encouraged to supplement the Student Interview Record with these provided questions, to reword these questions, and to create other questions to help in rating the FAAB components.

COMPONENT 1. INSTRUCTIONAL MATCH

1. Does your teacher know what things you are good at?
2. If you are having trouble with an assignment, does your teacher help you or give you something you are better able to do?

COMPONENT 2. INSTRUCTIONAL EXPECTATIONS

1. Does your teacher call on you in class?
2. Do you answer questions in class?
3. Does your teacher expect you to get good grades?
4. Does your teacher think everyone can do well in school? Does your teacher treat all students as if they can learn?
5. Do you know what the teacher expects of you?
6. What happens if you don't do what the teacher wants?

COMPONENT 3. CLASSROOM ENVIRONMENT

1. Do you know the rules in your classroom?
2. Do most students follow the teacher's rules?
3. What does your teacher do if you do something wrong?
4. Do you go to your teacher for help if you need it?
5. Are you busy working all day or do you have a lot of free time?
6. Do you know what to do when you finish your work? What do you do when you finish your work?
7. Does your teacher like you to participate in the classroom?
8. Do kids in the class help each other out?
9. Do you like being in this class?
10. Do all students get a chance to speak in class?

Student

COMPONENT 4. INSTRUCTIONAL PRESENTATION

1. Does your teacher explain things so that everyone understands?
2. Does your teacher make sure you understand the lesson before you work on your own?
3. Does your teacher make sure you've learned something before moving on to something new?
4. While you are working, does your teacher check your work to make sure you're doing it right and that you understand?
5. Does your teacher tell you what he/she's going to teach before he/she starts teaching?
6. Are your teacher's directions easy to follow and understand?
7. Do you ask your teacher questions when you don't understand?
8. Does your teacher tell you what you are going to learn on an assignment?
9. Does your teacher explain how to figure out a problem?
10. Does your teacher teach you how to learn different things?

COMPONENT 5. COGNITIVE EMPHASIS

1. If you don't understand something, does your teacher tell you the answer or help you figure it out yourself?
2. Do you know any strategies or "tricks" to make this assignment easier?

COMPONENT 6. MOTIVATIONAL STRATEGIES

1. Are your teacher's lessons interesting?
2. Do you do the same thing every day or do you get to try to do all different things?
3. Are you able to do your work?
4. Are your assignments too easy or too hard?
5. What does your teacher do if you do all your work correctly?
6. Are students rewarded for doing good work in your class?
7. Does your teacher know what your favorite things are to do?
8. Does your teacher say nice things about your work?

COMPONENT 7. RELEVANT PRACTICE

1. Do you have enough time to finish all of your work?
2. Is your work related to what your teacher teaches you?
3. Does your teacher check your work when you are working alone?
4. Do you ask your teacher for help if you don't understand?
5. Do you have enough time to practice new things you learn?
6. Do you work hard when you are working alone?
7. Do you have enough work to do?

FUNCTIONAL
ASSESSMENT OF
ACADEMIC
BEHAVIOR

Student

COMPONENT 8. INFORMED FEEDBACK

1. Does your teacher tell you how well you are doing?
2. Does your teacher help you when you do things wrong?
3. Does your teacher help you correct your mistakes?
4. If you make a mistake, does your teacher explain why what you did was wrong?
5. Do you know what you need to do better in?
6. If you don't understand something, does your teacher explain it again or in a different way?

COMPONENT 9. ACADEMIC ENGAGED TIME

1. Does your teacher keep you busy working?
2. If you finish your work before other students, does your teacher give you other things to do?
3. Do you get to answer as many questions as the other students?
4. Do you get to ask your teacher as many questions as you'd like?
5. If your teacher asks you a question and you don't know the answer, does he/she help you figure out the answer or does he/she ask somebody else?
6. Do you pay attention when your teacher is teaching something?
7. Do you know what to do when you finish your work? What do you do when you are finished with your work?
8. Does your teacher make sure you are doing your work?

COMPONENT 10. ADAPTIVE INSTRUCTION

1. Does your teacher try to explain things many different ways?
2. If you don't understand something, does your teacher go slower or explain it in a different way?
3. Do you know what things you need to learn how to do better?
4. Does your teacher try hard to help students who don't understand their work?

COMPONENT 11. PROGRESS EVALUATION

1. Do you learn a lot in school?
2. When everyone is working alone, does your teacher walk around and make sure everyone understands and is doing what they're supposed to?
3. Does your teacher ask you if you understand what you're doing?
4. Do you know how well you are doing in class?
5. Are you able to check your work by yourself?
6. Does your teacher go over things you already know before teaching you something new?

FUNCTIONAL
ASSESSMENT OF
ACADEMIC
BEHAVIOR

COMPONENT 12. STUDENT UNDERSTANDING

1. Do you know why the teacher teaches you certain things?
2. What happens if your work is not good enough?
3. Do you understand how to do your work?
4. Do you understand the directions your teacher gives you?
5. Do you know things to do to help you finish your work better?

References and Resources

Algozzine, B., & Ysseldyke, J. (Eds.) (1995). *Tactics for improving parenting skills*. Longmont, CO: Sopris West.

Algozzine, B. (1993). *50 simple ways to make teaching more fun*. Longmont, CO: Sopris West.

Algozzine, B., Ysseldyke, J., & Elliott, J. (1997). *Strategies and tactics for effective instruction*. 2nd ed. Longmont, CO: Sopris West.

America Goes Back to School: Parents Activity Guide (Obtain from the Institute of the Family Involvement Partnership for Learning, [800] USA-LEARN.)

Bandura, A. (1978). The self system in reciprocal determination. *American Psychologist, 33,* 344-358.

Beck, R., & Conrad, D. (1997). *Basic skill builders program*. Longmont, CO: Sopris West.

Beck, R. (1993). *Project RIDE: Responding to individual differences in education*. Longmont, CO: Sopris West.

Becker, W. C. (1971). *Parents are teachers: A child management program*. Champaign, IL: Research Press.

Berla, N., Garlington, J., & Henderson, A. (1993). *Taking stock: The inventory of family, community, and school support for students*. Washington, DC: National Committee for Citizens in Education.

Bickel, W. E. (1999). The implications of the effective schools literature for school restructuring. In C. R. Reynolds & T. B. Gutkin (Eds.), *The Handbook of School Psychology* (pp. 959-983). New York: John Wiley & Sons.

Binns, K., Steinberg, A., & Amorosi, S. (1997). *The Metropolitan Life Survey of the American Teacher 1998: Building Family-School Partnerships: Views of Teachers and Students*. New York: Louis Harris and Associates.

Bowen, J., Olympia, D., & Jenson, W. (1996). *Study buddies: Parent tutoring tactics*. Longmont, CO: Sopris West.

Braaten, S. (1999). *Behavioral objective sequence*. Champaign, IL: Research Press.

Bronfenbrenner, U. (1979). *The ecology of human development*. Cambridge:, MA: Harvard University Press.

Brophy, J. E., & Good, T. L. (1986). Teacher behavior and student achievement. In M. L. Wittrock (Ed.), *Handbook of research on teaching* (3rd ed.) (pp.328-375). New York: Macmillan.

Calfee, R. C. (1981). The reading diary: Acquisition of decoding. *Reading Research Quarterly, 16(3)*, 346-371.

Canter, A., & Carroll, S. (Eds.) (1998). *Helping children at home and school: Handouts from your school psychologist*. Bethesda, MD: National Association of School Psychologists.

Carroll, J. B. (1963). A model for school learning. *Teachers college Record, 64*, 723-733.

Chall, J. S. (2000). *The academic achievement challenge: What really works in the class-room?* New York: Guilford Press.

Chrispeels, J., Boruta, M., & Daugherty, M. (1988). *Communicating with parents*. San Diego, CA: San Diego County Office of Education. (6401 Linda Vista Rd., San Diego, CA 92111-7399)

Christenson, S. L. (2000). Families and schools: Rights, responsibilities, resources, and relationship. In R. C. Pianta & M. J. Cox (Eds.), *The Transition to kinder-garten* (143-177). Baltimore, MD: Brookes Publishing Co.

Christenson, S. L., & Christenson, C. J. (1998). *Family, school, and community influ-ences on children's learning: A literature review*. All Parents Are Teachers Project. Minneapolis, MN: University of Minnesota Extension Service.

Christenson, S. L., & Buerkle, K. (1999). Families as educational partners for chil-dren's school success: Suggestions for school psychologists. In C. R. Reynolds & T. B. Gutkin (Eds.), *Handbook of school psychology* (709-744). New York: Wiley & Sons.

Christenson, S. L., & Sheridan, S. L. (2001). *Schools and families: Creating essential connections for learning*. New York: Guilford Press.

Christenson, S. L., Rounds, T., & Gorney, D. (1992). Family factors and student achievement: An avenue to increase students' success. *School Psychology Quarterly, 1(3)*, 178-206.

Clark, R. M. (1983). *Family life and school achievement*. Chicago: University of Chicago Press.

Clark, R. M. (1990, Spring). Why disadvantaged students succeed: What happens outside of school is critical. *Public Welfare*, 17-23.

Cutright, M. J. (1989). *The national PTA talks to parents: How to get the best education for your child*. New York: Doubleday.

Decker, L. E. (1994). *Home/school/community relations: Trainers manual and study guide*. Mid-Atlantic Center for Community Education, Charlottesville, VA: University of Virginia.

Deshler, D., Shumaker, J., Bulgren, J., and others. (2001). Making learning easier: Connecting new knowledge to things students already know. *Teaching Exceptional Children, 33*, 82-85.

Elliott, J., Algozzine, B., & Ysseldyke, J. (1998) *Timesavers for educators*. Longmont, CO: Sopris West.

Epstein, J. L., Coates, L., Salinas, K. C., Sanders, M. G., & Simon, B. S. (1997). *School, family, and community partnerships: Your handbook for action*. Thousand Oaks, CA: Corwin Press, Inc.

Ferguson, S., & Mazin, L. (1989). *Parent power*. New York: Clarkson N. Potter, Inc.

Fischer, C. W., & Berliner, D. C. (Eds.) (1985). *Perspectives on instructional time*. New York: Longman.

Fister, S., & Kemp, K. (1995). *TGIF: But what will I do on Monday?* Longmont, CO: Sopris West.

Fister, S., & Kemp, K. (1995). *Making it work on Monday*. Longmont, CO: Sopris West.

Freemen, R. L., & Smith, C. I. (2001). Functional assessment: Responding to challenging behavior. *Impact, 14*(1), 6-7.

Galloway, J., & Sheridan, S. M. (1994). Implementing scientific practices through case studies: Examples using home-school interventions and consultation. *Journal of School Psychology, 32*, 385-413.

Gary, W., Marburger, C. L., Hansen, B., & Witherspoon, R. (1996). *Family, school, community partnerships*. Center for the Revitalization of Urban Education. Washington, DC: National Education Assoication.

Gettinger, M. (1988). Analogue assessment: Evaluating academic abilities. In E. S. Shapiro, & T. R. Kratochwill (Eds.), *Behavioral assessment in schools* (pp. 247-289). New York: Guilford Press.

Gettinger, M., & Stoiber, K. C. (1999). Excellence in Teaching: Review of instructional and environmental variables. In C. R. Reynolds & T. B. Gutkin (Eds.), *The Handbook of School Psychology* (pp. 933-958). New York: John Wiley & Sons.

Greene, L. J. (1987). *Smarter kids*. New York: Fawcett Crest.

Greenwood, C., Delquadri, J., & Carta, J. (1997). *Together we can: Classwide peer tutoring to improve basic academic skills*. Longmont, CO: Sopris West.

Hansen, D. A., (1986). Family-school articulations: The effects of interaction rule mismatch. *American Educational Research Journal, 23*(4), 643-659.

FUNCTIONAL
ASSESSMENT OF
ACADEMIC
BEHAVIOR

Harry, B. (1992). *Cultural diversity, families, and the special education system: Communication and empowerment*. New York: Teachers College Press.

Heller, L. R., & Fantuzzo, J. W. (1993). Reciprocal peer tutoring and parent partnership: Does parent involvement make a difference? *School Psychology Review, 22*(3), 517-534.

Henderson, A. T., & Berla, N. (1994). *A new generation of evidence: The family is critical to student achievement*. Washington, DC: National Committee for Citizens in Education.

Hess, R. D., & Holloway, S. D. (1984). Family and school as educational institutions. In R. D. Parke, R. N. Emde, H. P. McAdoo, & G. P. Sackett (Eds.), *Review of child development research: Vol 7. The family* (pp. 179-222). Chicago: University of Chicago Press.

Howell, K. W. (1986). Direct assessment of academic performance. *School Psychology Review, 15*(3), 324-335.

Institute for Mental Health Initiatives. (1998). *Anger management for parents: The RETHINK method*. Champaign, IL: Research Press.

Johnson, S. K., & Johnson, C. D. (1994). *Monitoring Your Student's Educational Progress: Families and Schools Together*. Longmont, CO: Sopris West.

Kellaghan, T., Sloane, K., Alvarez, B., & Bloom, B. S. (1993). *The home environment and school learning: Promoting parental involvement in the education of children*. San Francisco: Jossey-Bass.

Kuepper, J. (1987). *Homework helper: A guide for parents offering assistance*. Education Media Corp.

Lentz, F. E., Allen, S. J., & Ehrhardt, K. E. (1996). The conceptual elements of strong interventions in school settings. *School Psychology Quarterly, 11*(2), 118-136.

Maeroff, G. I. (1989). *The school smart parent*. New York: Times Books.

Mallen, T. (1995). *Taking charge of your child's education: Nine steps to becoming a learning ally*. Seattle, WA: Acumen Press.

Marliave, R., & Filby, N. N. (1985). Success rate: A measure of task appropriateness. In C. W. Fischer & D. C. Berliner (Eds.), *Perspectives on instructional time* (pp. 217-235). New York: Longman.

Moles, O. C. (1993). *Building school-family partnerships for learning: Workshops for urban educators*. Washington, DC: Office of Educational Research and Improvement.

National PTA. (1998). *National standards for parent/family involvement programs*. Chicago: Author. Available: www.pta.org

National PTA. (2000). *Building successful partnerships: A guide for developing parent and family involvement programs.* Bloomington, IN: National Education Service.

Olympia, D., Jenson, W., & Hepworth-Neville, M. (1996). *Sanity savers for parents: Tips for tackling homework.* Longmont, CO: Sopris West.

Paine, S. C., Radicchi, J. A., Rosellini, L. C., Deutchman, L., & Darch, C. (1983). *Structuring your classroom for academic success.* Champaign, IL: Research Press.

Patterson, G. R. (1976). *Living with children: New methods for parents and teachers.* Champaign, IL: Research Press.

Ramey, C. T., & Ramey, S. L. (1998). Early intervention and early experience. *American Psychologist, 53*(2), 109-120.

Reschly, D. J., Tilly, III W. D., & Grimes, J. P. (2000). *Special education in transition: Functional assessment and noncategorical programming.* Longmont, CO: Sopris West.

Rhode, G., Jensen, W., & Reavis, K. (1992). *The tough kid book.* Longmont, CO: Sopris West.

Rich, D. (1988). *MegaSkills: How families can help children succeed in school and beyond.* Boston: Houghton-Mifflin.

Rogers, E. M. (1983). *Diffusion of innovations.* New York: Free Press.

Salvia, J., & Ysseldyke, J. (2001). *Assessment.* Boston: Houghton-Mifflin.

Seeley, D. S. (1985). *Education through partnership.* Washington, DC: American Enterprise Institute for Public Policy Research.

Sheridan, S. M. (1997). Conceptual and empirical bases of conjoint behavioral consultation. *School Psychology Quarterly, 12*, 119-133.

Sheridan, S. M., Kratochwill, T. R., & Bergan, J. R. (1996). *Conjoint behavioral consultation: A procedural manual.* New York: Plenum.

Sheridan, S. M., Kratochwill, T. R., & Elliott, S. N. (1990). Behavioral consultation with parents and teachers: Delivering treatment for socially withdrawn children at home and school. *School Psychology Review, 19*, 33-52.

Sheridan, S. M. (1998). *Why don't they like me?: Helping your child make and keep friends.* Longmont, CO: Sopris West.

Shure, M. B. (1996). *Raising a thinking child workbook: Teaching young children how to resolve everyday conflicts and get along with others.* Champaign, IL: Research Press.

Silberman, M. (1995). *When your child is difficult.* Champaign, IL: Research Press.

Slavin, R. E., Karweit, N. L., & Wasik, B. A. (1994). *Preventing early school failure: Research, policy, and practice.* Needham Heights, MA: Allyn & Bacon.

FUNCTIONAL
ASSESSMENT OF
ACADEMIC
BEHAVIOR

Sloane, H. N. (1987). *The good kid book: How to solve the 16 most common behavior problems*. Champaign, IL: Research Press.

Sloane, K. D. (1991). Home support for successful learning. In S. B. Silvern (Ed.), *Advances in reading/language research: Vol. 5. Literacy through family, community, and school interaction* (pp. 153-172). Greenwich, CT: JAI Press.

Solomon, A. M., & Grenoble, P. B. (1988). *Helping your child get top grades*. Chicago: Contemporary Books.

Sprick, R., & Howard, L. (1995). *The teacher's encyclopedia of behavior management*. Longmont, CO: Sopris West.

Sprick, R., Sprick, M., & Garrison, M. (1993). *Interventions: Collaborative planning for students at risk*. Longmont, CO: Sopris West.

Stainback, W., & Stainback, S. (1988). *How to help your child succeed in school*. New York: Meadowbrook.

Sugai, G., & Horner, R. H. (2000). Including the functional behavioral assessment technology in schools. *Exceptionality, 8*(3), 145-148.

Tyler, T. (1950). *Basic principles of curriculum and instruction*. Chicago: University of Chicago Press.

U.S. Department for Education supplies free materials on family involvement. Contact: www.ed.govwww.ed.gov or 800-USA-LEARN.

U.S. Department of Education (1997). *A compact for learning: An action handbook for school-family-community partnerships*. Washington, DC: U.S. Department of Education Partnership for Family Involvement in Education. (Online.). Available: www.ed.govwww.ed.gov

Vernon, A., & Al-Mabuk, R. H. (1995). *What growing up is all about: A parent's guide to child and adolescent development*. Champaign, IL: Research Press.

Walberg, H. J. (1984). Families as partners in educational productivity. *Phi Delta Kappan, 65*, 397-400.

Wikelund, K. R. (1990). *Schools and communities together: A guide to parent involvement*. Portland, OR: Northwest Regional Educational Laboratory.

Young, K. R., West, R., Smith, D., & Morgan, D. P. (1991). *Teaching self-management strategies to adolescents*. Longmont, CO: Sopris West.

Ysseldyke, J. E., & Elliott, J. (1999). Effective instructional practices: Implications for assessing educational environments. In C. R. Reynolds & T. B. Gutkin (Eds.). *The Handbook of School Psychology* (pp. 497-518). New York: John Wiley & Sons.

Ysseldyke, J. E., & Christenson, S. L. (1987). Evaluating students' instructional environments. *Remedial and Special Education, 8*(3), 17-24.

Ysseldyke, J. E., & Christenson, S. L. (2001). *Using what we know*. Longmont, CO: Sopris West.

Ysseldyke, J. E., & Christenson, S. L. (1993). *TIES-II: The instructional environment system*. Longmont: Sopris West.

Zins, J., & Kratochwill, T. (1993). *Handbook of consultation services for children*. San Francisco: Jossey-Bass.

FUNCTIONAL
ASSESSMENT OF
ACADEMIC
BEHAVIOR